MW00629677

Quick Trips

By Lynn Edge

Published by *The Birmingham News*

Design & layout by Lori Leath-Smith

Copyright 1995 © by Lynn Edge, Birmingham, AL
Maps copyrighted by The Birmingham News Co.

All rights reserved.

No part of this publication may be reproduced, stored in a retrieval system or transmitted, in any form or by any means, electronic, mechanical, photocopying, recording or otherwise without the written permission of the publisher.

TABLE OF CONTENTS

Alabama

Florida

Georgia

Dedication

For my father who always took great pride in my
accomplishments and never hesitated to tell me so.

He gave me a love of travel. After all, he taught me to
listen for the lullaby played by moving railroad cars.

He gave me a love of adventure. After all,
he got us "train-left in New York."

He graced the first 24 years of my pilgrimage.
I have missed his company on the past 24.

His life was too quick a trip.
His influence is an endless journey.

Photo credits

Those photos that do not belong to *The Birmingham News* are being published thanks to the kindness of those listed below who gave permission for their use.

Page 6—Alabama Bureau of Travel and Tourism
Page 9—*The Birmingham News*
Page 14—Lynn Edge
Page 17—*The Birmingham News*
Page 20—*The Birmingham News*
Page 23—Lynn Edge
Page 26—Lynn Edge
Page 29—Lynn Edge
Page 32—Southern Tours of Marion
Page 35—Lynn Edge
Page 38—Lynn Edge
Page 44—*The Birmingham News*
Page 47—*The Birmingham News*
Page 65—Panama City Beach Convention and Visitors Bureau
Page 68—*The Birmingham News*
Page 82—Innkeepers K.C. and Vern Bassham
Page 85—Lynn Edge
Page 91—*The Birmingham News*
Page 94—Lynn Edge
Page 97—Lynn Edge
Page 100—Tourist Division, Georgia Department of Industry and Trade
Page 103—Courtesy of the National Corvette Museum, Bowling Green, Ky.
Page 106—Columbus, Miss., Chamber of Commerce
Page 109—Courtesy of Ed Williford, French Camp, Miss.
Page 118—The Associated Press
Page 121—Lynn Edge
Page 133—Lynn Edge

Introduction

When I sat down with Carol Nunnelley several years ago to discuss a new column for *The Birmingham News*, I don't think either of us imagined that this column would take on a life of its own.

At the time, we both envisioned simple little stories about places within an easy drive of Birmingham—spots *The News'* readers could see on a weekend outing. We didn't know how much response these columns would get.

One outdoor adventure company received 200 calls from Birmingham the morning after it was the subject of a "Quick Trip."

A bed and breakfast owner booked 80 guests in two days and had the usage on the B&B's "800" number quadruple as the result of a mention in "Quick Trips."

The owner of a Tennessee attraction still has visitors arrive with a copy of a two-year-old "Quick Trip" in hand. "They always say, 'We saved this because when we read it we knew we would come here someday.'," she says.

I didn't realize how much of an effect it would have on my life, either.

Over those past five years, I've written a "Quick Trip" for almost every week and I've had the pleasure of discovering places I never would have found otherwise. I've met new people who have become my friends and I've once again been convinced that there are no people like Southerners when it comes to hospitality.

I also didn't know that I would be called upon to unearth "Quick Trips" I considered ancient. Readers have asked me to do so when they've misplaced those "Quick Trips" they meant to save.

Which leads me to the purpose of this book. I've chosen 52 of my favorite "Quick Trips" from the past five years. The readers' response has shown me that these are among their favorites, too.

Now they won't have to search through the "junk drawer" for columns they meant to save. They are right here, neatly bound and ready to toss in the car.

As you read them, keep two things in mind—the attractions listed aren't the only ones to see in any given place and the places to stay and places to eat aren't the only ones either. Each trip you make is your own discovery, you may find a new way to go, a quaint shop, a different place to stay, a hidden restaurant. That's part of the fun of travel.

I've updated these "Quick Trips," double-checked phone numbers and confirmed hours and admission costs. Of course—like life—attractions, restaurants and hotels always are changing. So I only can promise you that these were correct at the time the book went to press.

Remember my three rules of travel:
   1. Times given are for the time zone in which the city is located.
   2. Call before you go.
   3. Being lost sometimes is half the adventure.

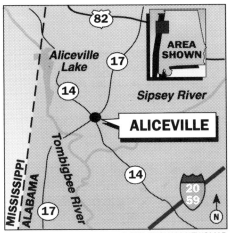

A BIRMINGHAM NEWSMAP

ALICEVILLE, ALABAMA

◉◉◉

The Prisoner of War Museum

"I often think on the days I spent in Alabama as a prisoner of war," the German soldier wrote in 1947. The letter addressed to the Mayor of Aliceville, where the soldier had been imprisoned, spoke fondly of the time spent in the South, in a place where he never lacked for food or clothes.

When Camp Aliceville was built, the people of the city had their doubts. "The people waited and watched for these fierce, savage people to arrive," recalled one resident. "Off the train came a group of young...innocent looking boys...Many of them looked not over 16 years of age."

Soon the residents learned that not only were the prisoners young, but they also were very different from what they had expected. Most of the men were from Rommel's Afrika Korps, a very cultured and educated group of soldiers.

The men who came to Camp Aliceville mostly were artisans —sculptors, writers, painters, musicians. And the fact that they were in prison in a strange place didn't suppress the urge to create something beautiful.

They painted and sketched, they sculpted, they landscaped, they organized acting companies, they published newspapers, they held classes in everything from blacksmithing to classical languages.

The POWs made their own marionettes and wrote plays for

1

them to perform. They built a 1,000-seat amphitheater out of hand-made bricks. One prisoner created a working violin out of matchsticks.

Because they could not take these things back to Germany when they left, Aliceville became the repository for all sorts of art pieces.

Today, many of those pieces—along with displays of and artifacts from Camp Aliceville—have a new home, the Aliceville Museum and Cultural Arts Center.

Housed in what once was the Coca-Cola Bottling Works, the museum opened Phase I in 1995. Later expansion will add a recreation of the 1940 bottling plant, a children's hands-on museum, a gallery for fine arts and an exhibit on the history of the Aliceville area.

The museum is open from 9 a.m. to 4 p.m. Tuesday through Friday. Admission is $3 for adults and $2 for children.

More to See and Do

James McCrory Gravesite. McCrory, Revolutionary War soldier and George Washington's bodyguard at Valley Forge, is buried in Bethany Cemetery near Aliceville. The cemetery is located a few miles west of Alabama 14, southeast of Aliceville.

How to Get There

Aliceville is located near the Alabama-Mississippi border on Alabama 14, about 34 miles southeast of Columbus, Miss.

Where to Stay

Voyager Motel.

WillowBrooke. A bed and breakfast.

Myrtlewood. A bed and breakfast.

Camping is available at Cochrane Campground or Pickensville Campground.

Where to Eat

The New Plantation House Restaurant. Set in an early1900s home, the restaurant serves down-home cooking. Open for lunch Tuesday through Sunday and for dinner Thursday through Saturday.

Broad Street Bistro. A new eatery to Aliceville, the Bistro features deli selections. Open every day for lunch, weekends for dinner.

Barry's Place. It's a 50's-style short-order restaurant. And it's popular with the local folks. Go early, there can be as much as a 30-minute wait for lunch. Serves lunch and dinner every day except Sunday and Wednesday.

For More Information

For more information about Aliceville, call 1-205-373-2820.

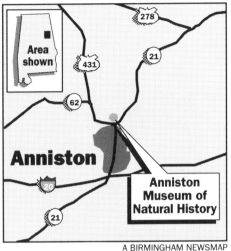

A BIRMINGHAM NEWSMAP

ANNISTON, ALABAMA

◉◉◉

Anniston Museum of Natural History

Walk into the cave and let your eyes become accustomed to the cool darkness. You can hear the dripping of water nearby as a hidden supply forms waterfalls and puddles.

Overhead, there are sleeping bats and in front of you stretch pathways that seem to wind farther and farther under the earth.

Then you remember, you're not underground at all. It's part of the magic created by the environment at the Anniston Museum of Natural History.

The cave is part of the museum's newest exhibit, Underground Worlds, in the Dynamic Earth Hall. Caves like this one exist all over Alabama, formed over millions of years of geological history.

This one didn't take quite that long. It took about 50 people five years to complete the museum's version. Along the way, they used a mile of steel, 59 tons of sand, 10,000 pounds of plaster and papier-mache and 1,500 plastic drinking straws. When they finished, the steel, plaster, sand and straws all went together to form realistic copies of cave walls, stalactites and stalagmites.

The Dynamic Earth Hall is one of several in the museum. Another, "Versatile Adapter," contains two ancient Egyptian mummies.

"East African Savannah" recreates that part of the world with displays of both plant and animal life and "Attack and Defense"

4

shows how various species protect themselves.

The "Designs for Living" Hall contains the heart of the exhibit, the Regar-Werner Ornithology exhibit. This exhibit once was the entire museum. The rest of it has grown around this extensive collection.

Each Hall has its own specially commissioned piece of art work and there is an art gallery in the museum as well.

Another addition to the museum is the Wildlife Garden, planted and designed to attract native wildlife. Throughout the garden, there are paved pathways and places for visitors to sit and enjoy the surroundings.

The museum is open from 9 a.m. to 5 p.m. Tuesday through Friday, from 10 a.m. to 5 p.m. on Saturday and from 1 to 5 p.m. on Sunday. Admission is $3 f or adults (18 and over) and $2 for children ages 4 to 17.

More to See and Do

The Church of St. Michael and All Angels. The Romantic Romanesque structure, built in 1888, is made entirely of Alabama marble. Especially notable is the 12-foot-long white marble altar. The church is open to touring visitors, except when there is a service going on, from 9 a.m. to 4 p.m.

Coldwater Covered Bridge. The bridge has been moved from its original site and re-installed near the Oxford Civic Center. It was built prior to 1850 and is one of more than a dozen restored covered bridges in the state.

How to Get There

The Anniston Museum of Natural History, is about two miles north of Anniston at the intersection of U.S 431 and Alabama 21.

Where to Stay

Hampton Inn, Oxford. Non-smoking rooms available.

Holiday Inn, Oxford. Non-smoking rooms available.

The Victoria. Some rooms set in an 1888 historic house.

Camping is available at Noccalula Falls Park, Gadsden.

Where to Eat

House of Chen. Chinese cuisine. Near the museum. Recommended by local diners.

Top O' The River. Catfish is the specialty. Open for dinner weekdays, lunch and dinner Sunday.

The Victoria. An elegant dining experience in a historic home.

For More Information

For more information about the museum, call 1-205-237-6766.

Realistic wildlife exhibit at Anniston Museum of Natural History

DELTA, ALABAMA

☉☉☉

Cheaha State Park

Yes, Virginia, there are mountains in Alabama. Often it seems that people who live north of the Mason-Dixon line think of the state in the same way man once thought of the earth—flat and not worth exploring.

Like those early notions of the earth, images of Alabama being mountainless and dull fade when someone takes the time to venture in and have a look around.

One of the best spots to have that look from may be Mount Cheaha, Alabama's highest point. The mountain, which rises more than 2,000 feet above sea level, is in Cheaha State Park. In addition to offering just about the best view in the whole state, the park also has thousands of acres of forest, woodland and foothills.

Of course, with the mountain standing so far above everything else, it isn't hard to spot—and apparently that has been the case for a long time. The area is mentioned in journals written by Hernando DeSoto during his 1540 expedition.

DeSoto and his men probably didn't find the accommodations atop the mountain quite as comfortable as they are now. The lodge and chalets in the park offer breathtaking views of the valley below.

Not quite as lush, but still comfortable are stone cabins built in the park with Civilian Conservation Corps labor. The men did good work—the cabins still are sturdy and secure.

For those who like the relive the days of DeSoto, there are camping facilities and a lake in the park as well.

Whether you stay at one of the park facilities or not, you can get a look at the miles and miles of Alabama that spread around the bottom of the mountain from the observation tower at the top. The tower also is a result of the CCC.

Many people come to the park to do more than just look. They like to sort of fade into the forest. Within the park is the Cheaha Wilderness, which covers the southernmost extension of the Appalachian Mountain Range.

More than 1,000 of the acres included in the wilderness are at least 2,000 feet above sea level, so there are plenty of chances for sweeping views of East Central Alabama along the hiking and backpacking trails.

More to See and Do

Clay County Courthouse. On the square in Ashland, this 1906 structure has the distinction of being the Alabama courthouse located at the highest point above sea level.

Socapatoy Covered Bridge. On Highway 77 in Waldo, this bridge was built in 1858.

How to Get There

Cheaha State Park is located in east central Alabama off U.S. 431 on Alabama 49.

Where to Stay

If the facilities at the park are full, try these nearby locations:

The Victoria, Anniston. Combines historic structure with new addition for the best of both worlds.

Holiday Inn, Oxford. Non-smoking rooms available.

Hampton Inn, Oxford. Non-smoking rooms available.

Where to Eat

Red's Catfish Cabin. Eight miles south of Lineville off Highway 49. Open Thursday and Friday for dinner, Saturday and Sunday for lunch and dinner.

Lee's Country Kitchen. Located on Highway 9 in Lineville. Features home-style cooking.

For More Information

For more information about Cheaha State Park, call 1-205-488-5115.

Visitors enjoy cool breezes and spectacular views from Alabama's highest point

9

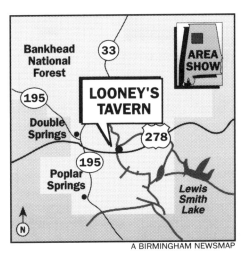

A BIRMINGHAM NEWSMAP

DOUBLE SPRINGS, ALABAMA

⊗⊗⊗

It is obvious that no one at the Twelve Oaks barbecue in Gone With The Wind was from Winston County, Ala. While all the men at that gathering were anxious to go to war and defeat the Union, the people in Winston County felt differently.

These people of northwest Alabama wanted to leave the two sides to fight it out among themselves. They didn't want to be a part of the war at all. That wasn't to be, however, and many of the men found themselves jailed as traitors to the Confederate cause.

Each year, the story of how Winston County became the "Free State of Winston" is told in an outdoor musical drama. The play tells the story of the historic July 4, 1862, meeting at Looney's Tavern and the events that meeting set into motion.

"The Incident at Looney's Tavern" opens at Looney's Tavern Amphitheater and Theme Park near Double Springs in early summer and continues through mid-fall each year.

What now is an entertainment complex began as just the amphitheater and the outdoor drama. Today it has expanded to include a 300-seat indoor theater, a riverboat, shops, restaurants and a miniature golf course.

The indoor theater houses live Nashville-style bands each day the outdoor drama is presented.

Looney Putt, the miniature golf course with a Civil War flavor, is open during the summer season.
Looney's Riverboat takes passengers cruising on Smith Lake. The paddle-wheel replica often has storytellers on board to weave tales of local history.
Cruises are scheduled for the dates the outdoor drama is presented.

How to Get There

Looney's Tavern Amphitheater and Theme Park is 29 miles west of Cullman on U.S. 278.

Where to Stay

Days Inn, Jasper. Non-smoking rooms available.

Holiday Inn, Hamilton. Non-smoking rooms available.

Camping is available at Clear Creek Campgrounds in the Bankhead Forest.

Where to Eat

Sister Sarah's Kitchen. On the grounds of the entertainment complex. All-you-can-eat buffet.

Della's Deli On the grounds of the entertainment complex.

For More Information

For more information about the entertainment complex or the outdoor drama, call 1-205-489-5000.

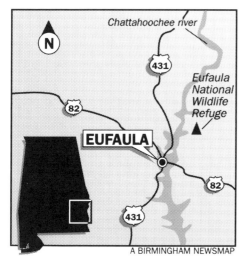

A BIRMINGHAM NEWSMAP

EUFAULA, ALABAMA

❂ ❂ ❂

The melody of "The Eufaula Waltz" drifts down the halls of Shorter Mansion in the city that gave the tune its name. It's played on a rosewood piano with mother-of-pearl keys and an inlaid decoration on the front.

As with most things Southern, there's a story that goes with the song. According to local historians, "The Eufaula Waltz" was composed in the 1860's and was dedicated to a Miss Carrie Caruthers.

There's a story that a blind man used to stand on the side of one of the streets passing the mansion and play the tune on his accordion.

Whether the story is true or not, such romantic notions as a blind man writing tunes for his lost love seem appropriate in Eufaula, a town that is the Deep South as people know it in books and movies.

It is a city of lovely old homes set against the backdrop of azaleas and dogwoods. It even comes complete with a river and Spanish moss hanging from the trees that line it.

And Eufaula truly is a town born of the trademark of the South—cotton. The city sits on a bluff above the Chattahoochee River and offers water access to Alabama, Georgia and Florida. In the early days of the town, steamboats regularly docked there to take on bales of cotton.

The crop made many early Eufaulians well-to-do and they built homes to reflect their wealth.

Shorter Mansion, one of those homes, and several other buildings in the Seth Lore Historic District are well-preserved reminders of the time when cotton was king.

Captain Seth Lore laid out the town of Irwinton (which became Eufaula) and the historic district honors him. It isn't hard to find the historic district if you remember the name. L-O-R-E. The district consists of Livingston Avenue, Orange Avenue, Randolph Avenue and Eufaula Avenue.

A walking/driving tour of the district and several other historic districts in the city is available from The Eufaula Heritage Association, 340 North Eufaula Ave.

More to See and Do

Eufaula National Wildlife Refuge. A dual land use area, the refuge is farmed during the growing season and flooded during the migratory seasons to provide a resting place for birds making their annual journeys to and from the south.

Tom Mann Fish World. Fish World is the home of one of the world's largest bass aquariums. Call ahead and find out about feeding times. Bass, it turns out, have very good appetites. Also at Fish World is the plant where Mann's company produces fishing lures.

At one time, all of the lures were personally approved by Leroy Brown, Mann's "pet" bass. If Leroy would nip at a lure, it would go into production; if he ignored it, the lure wasn't worth the trouble to market. Leroy's gone now, but there's a monument to him on the grounds at Fish World.

The Tavern. This building, on the bluff overlooking Lake Eufaula, was constructed in the 1830's to accommodate Chattahoochee River traffic. It's been a tavern and a Confederate hospital and now serves as a business/residence. The Tavern is believed to be Eufaula's oldest frame structure.

How to Get There

Eufaula is in southeast Alabama on U.S. 431.

Where to Stay

Holiday Inn. Non-smoking rooms available.

Lakepoint Resort State Park. Cabins and resort motel rooms. Tennis, golf, swimming pool.

Camping, is available at Lakepoint Resort State Park.

Where to Eat

Chewalla Restaurant. Serves breakfast, lunch and dinner. Family atmosphere.

Dogwood Inn. Set in 1905 home. Serves lunch and dinner, Monday through Saturday.

For More Information

For more information about Eufaula, call the Chamber of Commerce, 1-334-687-6664.

One of Eufaula's antebellum homes, open for tours

EUFAULA, ALABAMA

◉◉◉

Kendall Manor

Timothy and Barbara Lubsen had a dream—they wanted to open a bed and breakfast. They were living in Atlanta and had looked at possible bed and breakfast properties in Virginia and Georgia.

On one of those "shopping" trips, they drove back through Eufaula. "We drove up the hill and were in awe of so many charming older homes," Barbara said. "Then we saw Kendall Manor and we just pulled over to the curb and stared!

"Then we noticed a 'For Sale' sign and one saying it was a bed and breakfast. Tim said I was out of the car in 10 seconds. The rest is history and we have the feeling it was just meant to be."

Timothy and Barbara bought the home and once again have it up and running as a bed and breakfast, giving their guests a look at the elegance of Alabama's past.

James Turner Kendall came to Eufaula in the early 1850's and, before too long, chose a spot on a hilltop for his family's home. Construction on the house may have begun before the Civil War, but the home wasn't completed until 1872, at a cost of more than $30,000.

Kendall got a lot for his money, however. The two-story Italiante home had double parlors, six bedrooms and a dining room. The formal entrance to the home was through double doors of walnut with transom and side lights of ruby colored glass. All

15

of the rooms had fireplaces with mantels of Italian marble.

The open porch that surrounds three sides of the house has 52 columns. There is a scroll design at the top of each column and all 52 are said to have been carved by the same man.

The home's crowning glory, however, is the belvedere, set in slender columns with arched windows and plastered walls. Even though there are 100 steps from the driveway to the belvedere, many guests at Kendall have said the view alone is well worth the walk.

They've also gotten a glance into Kendall family history at the end of the climb. Members of the family obviously made a habit of going to the belvedere and writing poems or just their names and a date on the walls for more than 100 years. One of the visitors' favorites is "I, Joe Kendall, came up here on Sunday, January 15, 1905, to keep from going to church with my mother."

Six generations of Kendalls occupied the home and 10 Kendall brides were married there.

In fact, some of those Kendalls may still be around. "The ghost stories that have been passed down through the years serve to keep the spirit—as well as the spirits—of the house intact," Barbara said.

More to See and Do

Fairview Cemetery. The iron fence that surrounds the cemetery once was in place at the Union Female College. Buried here are European settlers, Confederate soldiers and slaves.

How to Get There

Eufaula is in southeast Alabama on U.S. 431.

Where to Stay

Lakepoint Resort State Park. Cabins and resort motel rooms. Tennis, golf, swimming pool.

Best Western—Eufaula Inn. Non-smoking rooms available.

Camping is available at Lakepoint Resort State Park.

Where to Eat

Anchor Inn. Serve dinner Tuesday through Saturday.

Creek Restaurant. Specializes in steak, seafood, catfish. Casual atmosphere.

For More Information

For information about Kendall Manor, call 1-334-687-8847. For more information about Eufaula, call 1-334-687-6664.

Eufaula's Kendall Manor has its own ghost

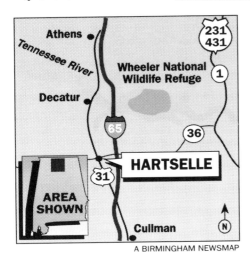

A BIRMINGHAM NEWSMAP

HARTSELLE, ALABAMA

◉ ◉ ◉

In 1992, Hartselle was chosen one of "The 100 Best Small Towns in America" in a book written by Norman Crampton, a former Chicago Sun-Times reporter.

Crampton made his choices based on "quality of life" and growth of the city. Hartselle made the cut after the author looked at location, crime rate, cost of living and a number of other things.

Of course, if Crampton had been making his choices in the early 1900s, he might have had to bypass Hartselle. In the early morning hours of March 15, 1926, a tale of "dastardly" (as those who tell the story describe it) crime began to unfold in the city.

Fifteen bank robbers crept into the city and cut the three telephone cables linking Hartselle to the rest of the world. Then they went to the Bank of Hartselle and set off eight blasts of nitroglycerin.

The robbers made off with all the cash and gold in the bank along with some of its silver coins. The only injury during the incident was to a dentist who hurt his leg as he ran into the street thinking he was responding to a fire alarm.

The bank was open, thanks to some help from other banks in the city, the next day. In fact, it soon was enjoying more business than it ever had before the robbery. As for the bandits, they never were caught or identified.

It isn't the site of the infamous heist that brings people to

Hartselle today, however. Antique shoppers are coming to the city to enjoy its newest attraction—antique shops and malls.

The city has 11 antique shops, several antique malls and one large antique and estate auction house.

"We want to become a tourist shopping hot spot," says Connie Bolton of the city's Chamber of Commerce.

One of the stores, which stretch along Main Street, U.S. 31, Railroad Street and Thompson Road, is open seven days a week.

Others have hours and days open that vary—sometimes according to the whim of the owner.

The Chamber of Commerce can provide shoppers with a map and a guide to store hours.

More to See and Do

Sparkman Park. Near the center of the city, the 80-acre park has basketball courts, tennis courts, a walking trail and carpet golf as well as playgrounds and places to picnic.

Wheeler Wildlife Refuge. One of the state's largest wildlife refuges, Wheeler is the wintering ground of a large number of waterfowl and home to several species of animal and plant life.

How to Get There

Hartselle is located in north Alabama, about 70 miles north-west of Birmingham off I-65 on U.S. 31.

Where to Stay

Windwood Inn.

Holiday Inn, Decatur. Non-smoking rooms available.

Amberley Suite Hotel, Decatur. Non-smoking rooms available.

Camping is available at Point Mallard Park, Decatur.

Where to Eat

Carol Anne's Corner Cafe. A place to "catch up on the latest in Hartselle," according to local residents. Serves breakfast, lunch and dinner.

Whitt's Barbecue. Recommended by a number of residents. Serves lunch and dinner.

Roberts' Catfish Lodge. This catfish restaurant gets a "thumbs-up" from residents who ate there even before the lodge was open. Serves lunch and dinner.

For More Information

For more information about Hartselle, call 1-205-773-4370.

Old Hartselle Tabernacle dates back to the 19th Century

Central Huntsville

ALABAMA
CONSTITUTION
VILLAGE

Area
shown

A BIRMINGHAM NEWSMAP

HUNTSVILLE, ALABAMA

◉◉◉

Alabama's Constitution Village

When a lesson in early Alabama history is in order, there's no better place to go for it than Alabama's Constitution Village, the living history museum that commemorates the birthplace of the state.

A walking tour of the complex, with its recreated Federal period buildings, starts in Constitution Hall, a working 19th century cabinetmaker's shop. It was here that the 44 delegates from the Alabama Territory met to write the state's first constitution in 1819.

When the delegates got to the city, they found the two-story frame building was the only one large enough to accommodate them.

The structure that had built frames for furnishings found it had become the spot for framing the future of the state.

Next on the tour is the Clement Clay Building, which houses Clement Clay's law office, Huntsville's first post office and the U.S. Surveyor General's office. A post riders' stable and a blacksmith shop are the next two stops.

After them, visitors see the outbuildings for the John Boardman building. The outbuildings housed slaves' quarters, apprentice's quarters and a kitchen.

In the John Boardman building next door are Alabama's first lending library and John Boardman's print shop, where the Alabama Republican newspaper and Alabama's first constitution were printed.

Next on the tour is the Stephen Neal Residence, home of Madison County Sheriff Neal and his family. It is a typical 19th-century middle class house with parlor, dining room, work area, bedroom and trunk room. On the grounds around the Neal House are the family garden, barn and "necessary house."

The final stop on the tour is the Neal kitchen. Typically, the kitchens of that day were located away from the main house. Kitchens often burned down and enterprising folk saw no need to let them take the main houses with them.

Alabama's Constitution Village is open Monday through Saturday from 9 a.m. to 5 p.m. March through December. Admission is $6 for adults, $5.50 for senior citizens (55 and over) and $3.50 for children (6-college).

More to See and Do

Maple Hill Cemetery. The cemetery dates from 1818 and is the burial place of many well-known Huntsville and Alabama citizens. Among them are five governors of Alabama, Confederate Secretary of War Leroy Pope Walker and the mother of actress Tallulah Bankhead.

How to Get There

Alabama's Constitution Village is in Huntsville at 109 Gates Avenue. From I-65, take U.S. 72 into Huntsville. From U.S. 72, turn south onto Washington Street. Take Washington to Gates.

Where to Stay

Amberley Suites Hotel. All-suite hotel. Non-smoking rooms available.

Hampton Inn. Free Continental breakfast. Non-smoking rooms available.

Stockton House. A bed and breakfast facility.

Camping is available at Monte Sano State Park.

Where to Eat

Cafe Berlin. Specialties are German dishes, with a wide assortment from which to choose. Desserts are excellent. Serves lunch and dinner daily.

Kountry Kitchen. Around the corner from Alabama's Constitution Village. Serves breakfast and lunch Monday through Friday

The Dogwood Cafe. Also near Alabama's Constitution Village. Serves breakfast, lunch and "snacks."

For More Information

For more information about Huntsville, call 1-800-SPACE-4-U.

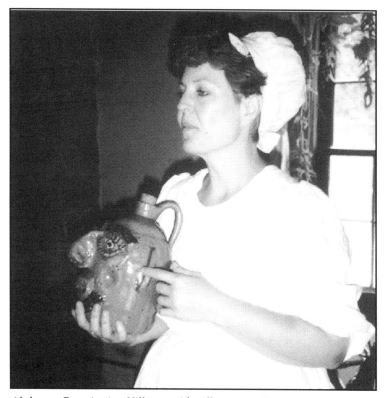

Alabama Constitution Village guide offers narrative on native household goods

23

SHELBY CO.

Area shown ■

Montevallo

25

155

Jemison

Union Grove

5

191

31

BIBB CO.

COOSA CO.

Clanton

65

22

PERRY CO.

CHILTON CO.

JEMISON, ALABAMA

◉◉◉

The Jemison Inn

Hunting and buying antiques has long been a passion for many collectors. Finding just the right thing at just the right price is on the level with winning Olympic gold in the world of antique lovers.

More and more antique lovers in the South are discovering one of Alabama's best kept secrets—an antique hunter's paradise with an antique-filled bed and breakfast to serve as home base.

And there's even an added bonus—the folks at the B&B know antiques. In fact, he owns an antique shop and she does antique appraising.

Joe and Nancy Ruzicka, owners of the Jemison Inn, have a quick answer for their guests who ask "What should we do today?" They give them a map of antique shops in the area and send them on their way.

Guests don't have to go out the front door to find a wealth of antiques, however. There are plenty to be seen in the inn itself. Joe's antique shop, Farm House Antiques, isn't far away and many pieces of the furniture in the B&B came from there. Other pieces came with the house, which was built in the 1930s.

The brick structure sitting in the heart of the Chilton County town was home to a Dr. McNeill, one of Jemison's early physicians.

With the Ruzickas' shared passion for antiques, it's not surprising to find out that the look of the house changes in subtle ways from time to time. "This chair doesn't really belong on the porch," Mrs. Ruzicka once said about a very "unporch-like" piece of furniture. "I just bought it today." The chair will find its way into the house eventually.

Since the inn is a bed and breakfast, a full breakfast comes with an overnight stay. "I tell my guests they can't stay more than seven nights because I would have to start repeating my breakfast menu," Mrs. Ruzicka laughs. "And I don't like to serve anyone the same thing more than once."

The inn, with three guest rooms, also is home to the Ruzickas, who have converted attic space into innkeepers' quarters. They've also added a deck and an in-ground swimming pool for their guests and themselves.

Rates at the Jemison Inn range from $55 to $60 per night. The Duffee Room has a double bed with private bath. The Johnson Room, with a double bed, and the McNeill Room, with twin beds, share a bath.

How to Get There
Jemison is southwest of Birmingham, off I-65. The Jemison Inn is on Highway 191, west of U.S. 31.

Where to Stay
If the Jemison Inn is booked up (and it frequently is), here are some other places to stay while antique hunting in Chilton County:

Key West Inn, Clanton.

Holiday Inn, Clanton.

Camping is available at Peach Queen Campground, Jemison.

Where to Eat
Heaton Pecan Farm, Clanton. Try the Pecan Chicken Salad here. Save room for the dessert (mostly ice creams featuring pecans) selection, too.

Country's Bar-B-Que. It's just plain good barbecue and you can choose how hot you want the sauce to be.

During peach season, treat yourself to dessert at any of the peach stands that fill Chilton County.

For More Information
For more information about the Jemison Inn, call 1-205-688-2055. For more information about Chilton County, call 1-205-755-2400.

The Jemison Inn, a bed and breakfast

It is a quiet place, serene almost to the point of being eerie. Spread over 102 acres of wooded Alabama countryside, Confederate Memorial Park was the site of the state's only Confederate veterans' home. It also is the final resting place of many of the men who spent their last days there.

One of the few cemeteries in the United States where only Confederate veterans are buried, the two burial areas at the park hold the graves of more than 200 veterans, 15 Confederate wives and the tomb of an Unknown Soldier.

MARBURY, ALABAMA

●●●

Confederate Memorial Park

The Alabama Confederate Soldiers Home came into being in 1901.

The next year, Jefferson Manley Falkner, a Montgomery attorney and Confederate veteran, gave 80 acres of his land as a site for the home. To raise money for the construction of the home, Falkner persuaded the young ladies of Montgomery to sell lecture tickets whose proceeds would benefit the project.

Falkner had hoped to raise about $500 this way. He underestimated the sales skills of the young ladies, however. They sold more than $7,000 worth of tickets.

Over the following year, a 22-building complex grew on the site and veterans came to live at the facility. The population of the home hit its peak during the First World War. After that, the number of residents dramatically fell.

In June 1934, the last veteran in residence died, leaving seven widows of veterans living in the home. The home was closed and the last five widows moved to other locations in 1934.

One by one, the buildings were torn down, leaving only their foundations and the two cemeteries to outline what once had been the sprawling site of cottages, a dairy, a hospital and a mess hall.

Today a museum set in a log cabin tells the story of the men who fought for the Confederacy and lived out their lives at the home.

Service records for the men who are buried in the cemeteries are housed there as well.

A driving and walking tour takes visitors through the complex, pointing out the sites of the buildings. Also on the tour are the sites of the elaborate water system and carbide gas system that supplied the cottages and other buildings at the home.

The two cemeteries, where the original markers have been cleaned and repaired, are open to visitors. New granite markers also have been installed at the foot of each grave. Among the notables buried at the site is James Wildcat Cater, an Indian herb and medicine man, who was one of the last veterans to come to the home.

The Park gates are open from dawn to dusk. The museum at the park is open from 9 a.m. to 5 p.m. daily.

More to See and Do

Lay Dam, Clanton. Guided tours of the hydroelectric generating plant are given on weekday afternoons and weekends.

How to Get There

Marbury and the Confederate Memorial Park, are off U.S. 231 on Alabama 23.

Where to Stay

Holiday Inn, Clanton. Non-smoking rooms available.

Camping is available at Peach Queen Campground, Jemison.

Where to Eat

Patsy's Kitchen, Marbury. The spot where all the locals go. Downhome cooking. Serves breakfast, lunch and dinner. Closed on Sunday.

Verbena Barbecue, Verbena. Serves lunch and dinner. Closed on Sunday.

For More Information

For more information about Confederate Memorial Park, call 1-205-755-1990.

Entrace to the Confederate Memorial Park near Marbury, Ala.

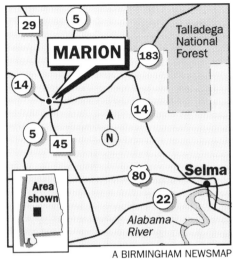

A BIRMINGHAM NEWSMAP

MARION, ALABAMA

◉◉◉

Women's Hall of Fame

They line the rooms, looking out over campus scenes, as they tell a silent story of some of Alabama's greatest citizens. Here, at Judson College, the state salutes her true Steel Magnolias—her women who have changed history and lives through the years.

They come from all walks of life, from all areas of endeavor. Their names read like a roll call of Who's Who— Helen Keller, Julia Tutwiler, Amelia Gorgas, Tallulah Bankhead, Lurleen Wallace, Zelda Fitzgerald.

The Hall of Fame, housed in A. Howard Bean Hall, was established in 1970. It recognizes women native to, or closely identified with, Alabama—women who has made significant contributions to the state, the nation and the world.

In most years, two more names are added to the list of honorees.

On three occasions, however, three inductees have been named. Hallie Farmer, Miss Keller and Miss Tutwiler were the first women to be chosen for the Hall of Fame. They were inducted in the first ceremony in 1971.

In 1991, sisters Virginia and Anna Praytor were inducted along with Julia Barron. The following year, Bessie Bellingrath was chosen along with the mother-daughter combination of Zelda Fitzgerald and "Scottie" Fitzgerald Smith.

Walking through the Hall of Fame is a trip through Alabama's history, seen through the eyes of the women who have helped give the state its character.

Because it is on a college campus, the Hall of Fame is open during school hours. There is no admission.

More to See and Do

Marion Military Institute Campus. Several buildings here are on the National Register of Historic Places. The Chapel was used as a Confederate hospital during the Civil War. A Friday visit might give guests an opportunity to see a marching drill.

Harry's Monument. This 1854 monument was erected to "Harry," a servant who died saving the lives of Marion Military Institute students during a fire.

Southern Tours of Marion. This relatively inexpensive tour service takes visitors past—and sometimes into—Marion's historic structures. If the group is large enough, lunch can be included.

How to Get There

Marion is in west Central Alabama off Alabama 5 on Perry County 4.

Where to Stay

The Gateway Inn. This newly opened facility is adjacent to the Gateway Inn Restaurant, a local favorite.

Myrtle Hill. A bed and breakfast facility.

Camping is available at Paul Grist State Park, near Selma.

Where to Eat

Gateway Inn. Open for lunch Sunday through Friday and dinner Monday, Wednesday, Friday and Saturday, this restaurant features seafood, catfish, crawfish, steaks and chicken.

Dale's Tearoom. In the center of the antique shops, Dale's offers "antiquers" a break for lunch on Wednesday, Thursday and Friday.

For More Information

For information about Southern Tours of Marion, call 1-334-683-6100.

Southern Tours of Marion specializes in old South charm

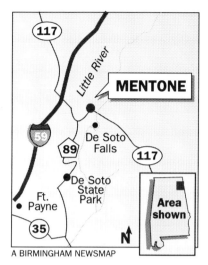

A BIRMINGHAM NEWSMAP

MENTONE, ALABAMA

◉ ◉ ◉

In the Gay Nineties, the northeast Alabama town of Mentone was a summer resort that drew visitors from all over the United States. Today, it seems to have developed a reputation as more of a fall getaway—a place to go and enjoy the changing colors of the leaves as they herald the coming of winter.

Whatever the season, the quaint little city has a lot to offer visitors who are looking for a change of pace and a respite from the hectic pace of day-to-day life.

Things seem to move a bit slower in Mentone, but no one seems to mind.

A good beginning spot for seeing the town is most imposing structure in the city—the Mentone Springs Hotel. Built in 1884 by Frank Caldwell, who fell in love with the area when he visited a friend there, the hotel once advertised that the area's climate would make visitors "feel the 'Spirit of Youth' as you have not felt it for years."

Today, the structure with its turrets houses a restaurant. Next door, the White Elephant Galleries offers antiques, art, crafts and, from time to time, musical entertainment.

Diagonally across the street is The Gourdie Shop, filled with creations made from locally grown gourds. The Gourdies seem to live much the same kind of life that humans do and visitors will find them dressed for all sorts of occasions—from baseball games to weddings to holidays.

For visitors in the market for local crafts or antiques, the Hitching Post offers everything from birdhouses to pianos.

Nearby is St. Joseph's On The Mountain Church. The log structure that forms the central part of the church was built in 1826.

One word of warning - during the winter, some stores may close or may change their hours of operation. Check before you travel.

More to See and Do

Cloudmont Ski and Golf Resort and Shady Grove Dude and Guest Ranch. It's a ski resort if the weather cooperates. During the winter, if the temperature goes below 29 for a few nights, they turn on the snow machines and cover the ground with the white stuff. The next day, it's obvious the word has gotten out, because the slopes are covered with skiers. The rest of the year, it's a golf course with such challenges as a tee that's 30 feet above the fairway. The Dude Ranch also offers the opportunity for hayrides and horseback outings along the rim of DeSoto Falls.

Sallie Howard Memorial Chapel. Near DeSoto State Park, the church is built against a 20-foot tall boulder. The rock serves as the back wall of the structure and the pulpit is made from stone found in Little River. Services are held each Sunday and the church generally is open to visitors during the day.

DeSoto State Park. It's got just about everything visitors might be looking for in a mountain getaway. There are hiking trails, a river, a canyon, a nature center and a building with a big front porch and rocking chairs. Accommodations range from campsites to rooms in a resort lodge. There also are cabins and chalets.

How to Get There

Mentone is located off I-59 in North Alabama on Alabama 117.

Where to Stay

Quality Inn, Fort Payne. Non-smoking rooms available.

Madaperca B&B. A bed and breakfast facility located in the historic district of Mentone.

Woodhaven B&B, Valley Head. A bed and breakfast facility set on a working farm.

Camping is available at DeSoto State Park.

Where to Eat

Log Cabin Deli, Mentone. It's recommended for the Old South dishes, including home cooked vegetables, that are served. Try the signature beverage—the Cabin Coolor. Open Tuesday through Sunday from 11 a.m. to 9 p.m.

Dessie's Kountry Chef, Mentone. Catfish and fresh vegetables are the specialties here. Open Monday, Wednesday, Thursday and Friday from 10 a.m. to 9 p.m.; Saturday from 7 a.m. to 9 p.m. and Sunday from 11 a.m. to 2 p.m.

For More Information

For more information about Mentone, call 1-205-845-3957.

Mentone Hotel is a landmark in the mountains of northeast Alabama

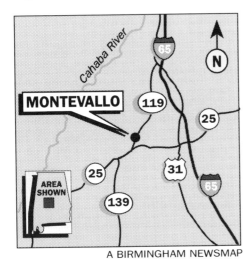

A BIRMINGHAM NEWSMAP

MONTEVALLO, ALABAMA

⊚ ⊚ ⊚

L ots of people go to the University of Montevallo to get an education. Lots of other people go there to look at the trees.

The campus has such a wide variety of trees, in fact, that the university has developed a "Tree Walk" that takes visitors around the shady walkways of the campus past 30 plants of interest. The guide also invites those who want to see other trees "up close" to wander off the marked trail and have a better look.

Among the trees along the way are:

1. Willow Oaks. The trail starts here with these narrow-leafed oaks that can be seen as the visitor stands with his back to Palmer Hall.

2. Sunburst Locust. A variety of honey locust, this tree is located by crossing the street in front of Palmer Hall and walking to the right corner of the grassy quadrangle.

3. Bur Oak. The large acorns this oak bears are among its most noticeable traits. You'll find this tree as you leave the Sunburst Locust and walk toward the flagpole.

4. Dahoon Holly. Found at the corner where the front and the east wing of Reynolds Hall meet, this holly is rare in Alabama except along streams and swamps in Mobile County.

5. Ginkgo. Simply turn around after finding the Dahoon Holly and find the tree with the fan-shaped leaves. It is the Ginkgo, the only survivor of a group of trees which long ago disappeared from

much of the earth. In the fall, the leaves are a beautiful yellow.

6. Chinese Tallow Tree. To find this tree, go toward the mini-park in front of Anna Irvin Hall. Enter the park via the flagstone walk on the left side of the park, turn left and go to the end. This tree came to the United States from China in the mid-1800s.

7. Bald Cypress. This tree, which sheds all its leaves in the fall, occurs naturally in swamps and river banks along the Coast. It is located near the rear corner of Hill House.

For a complete guide to the trees on campus, contact the Montevallo Chamber of Commerce.

More to See and Do

Exploring the Shops in Montevallo. Among the places to while away the time (and maybe find just the thing you're looking for) are The House of Serendipity, set in a building with a tin ceiling; Earthworks, featuring hand-made pottery; Studio of Kings, photography studio and shop belonging to trumpeter Chuck King and Too Much Java, a coffeehouse.

King House. The 1823 plantation structure, on the campus of the University of Montevallo, is said to still be home to ghosts of the original owners. It also houses special guests of the university.

Orr Park. Set along Shoal Creek, the park is home to the original cedar carvings of Tim Tingle. There also is a playground for the children and picnic tables for the grown-ups.

How to Get There

Montevallo is off I-65 on Alabama 25.

Where to Stay

Days Inn, Calera. Non-smoking rooms available.

Key West Inn, Clanton. Non-smoking rooms available.

Camping is available at Brierfield Ironworks.

Where to Eat

The Plaza Cafe. Among the specials on a recent menu were Five Cheese and Fresh Herb Manicotti with Marinara Sauce and Seafood Crepes with Shrimp Cream Sauce.

Firehouse Bar-B-Q. The menu includes barbecue by the pound and by the slab as well as boiled and grilled shrimp (on Friday and Saturday only). Serves lunch and dinner daily.

JeRoes. A local meeting place at lunch. Home-cooked meats and vegetables are served from the buffet.

For More Information

For more information about Montevallo, call 1-205-665-1519.

Stately hardwoods flanking this campus drive provide the college with old Southern charm

A BIRMINGHAM NEWSMAP

MONTGOMERY, ALABAMA

⊙⊙⊙

The Alabama Capitol

It seemed at times during the long restoration process that the work would go on forever, that there never would be an end to it and a reopening of Alabama's capitol.

There was an end to the work that began in 1986, however, and it was worth the wait. The newly reborn capitol is a treasure and visiting it is a joy.

The first capitol on the site was built in 1847. It was destroyed by fire two years later. The core of the building most Alabamians remember from their elementary school tours was built in 1850 on the same site.

A rear wing was added in 1885 and the two side wings came into being between 1906 and 1912.

It was this building that was beginning to show its considerable age when the restoration efforts began. And it is the beauty of that building that has emerged from the scaffolding and dust cloths that had covered it during the work that brought it back to life.

Now everything has the look of being new without really looking new. Pains were taken to bring the Capitol back to the building it once was instead of giving it a whole new look.

In fact, visitors can see just how the work was done. In several places throughout the building, portions of the original trompe l'oeil wall painting have been left in combination with the matching new decorative painting.

39

The Capitol remains a place of business. The governor comes to work here along with a number of other state officials and computers sit side-by-side with antiques as the state's affairs are carried out.

A brochure takes visitors on a self-guided tour through the building, explaining what each room was designed for and how the restoration was done. A souvenir booklet with color photographs of the Capitol costs only 50 cents and is well worth the price.

The Capitol is open from 9 a.m. to 4 p.m. Monday through Saturday.

More to See and Do

Scott and Zelda Fitzgerald Museum. Though the author and his wife lived here only a few months, the home is the only museum to the Fitzgeralds. A visit begins with a video about the couple's life. A trip through the rooms gives visitors a look at some of the couple's letters and other memorabilia. The museum is open from 10 a.m. to 2 p.m. Monday through Friday and from 1 to 5 p.m. on Saturday and Sunday. Admission is free, but a donation of $2 for adults and $1 for students is requested.

How to Get There

Montgomery is located in central Alabama on I-65.

Where to Stay

Riverfront Inn. Set in the former Montgomery freight depot. Non-smoking rooms available.

The Lattice Inn. A bed and breakfast.

Camping is available at Fort Toulouse/Jackson Park, Wetumpka.

Where to Eat

Dumplin's at The Elite. For years, The Elite actually was the seat of state government, with policies being discussed and agreements being reached over lunch here. It was a big blow to the city when the restaurant was closed a few years ago. Now its back with a little added to the name and the interior of the building restored and refurbished. A trolley (provided free by the restaurant) goes through the downtown area about every 15 minutes at lunch time to collect diners from the various office buildings and sites and take them to The Elite.

Terrace Cafe, Montgomery Museum of Art. The cafe serves lunch from 11 a.m. to 2 p.m. and the menu is varied, with several light dishes and refreshing desserts.

For More Information

For more information about Montgomery, call the Visitor Information Center (located in the historic district), 1-334- 262-0013.

The recently restored Alabama Capitol is a site of national historic significance

41

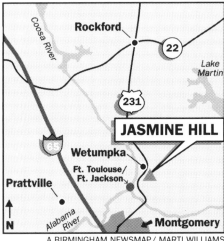

A BIRMINGHAM NEWSMAP/ MARTI WILLIAMS

MONTGOMERY, ALABAMA

◎◎◎

Jasmine Hill Gardens

With the excitement of the 1996 Summer Olympics in Atlanta, it's not surprising that people might seek out a taste of Greece, the country that gave birth to the Olympic Games.

For those in Alabama, the taste is only a few miles from the state Capitol in secluded gardens where the rest of the world seems very far away. That place, 17 acres filled with fine reproductions of classical Greek sculpture, is Jasmine Hill Gardens.

The gardens were a sort of creation of love—put together by Mary and Ben Fitzpatrick. The Fitzpatricks, who were married in 1907, were the owners of a chain of stores across the South. When they sold their holdings in 1927, they were able to retire to their own personal haven—Jasmine Hill.

There, they spent their time in the gardens reading poetry to one another. But they didn't spend all their time there. They also traveled, especially to Greece.

On their trips, they would commission copies of sculptures that they liked and return the next year to pick them up. They would set the sculptures up in the gardens at Jasmine Hill where flowers now abound year-round.

Also on the grounds is a copy of what remains of the Greek Temple of Hera, which sat in one of the most sacred precincts of ancient Greece, adjacent to the site of the Olympic games.

Jasmine Hill Gardens is open from 9 a.m. to 5 p.m. Tuesday through Sunday. Admission charge is $3.50 for adults, $2 for children 6-12. The gardens close for the winter. (Closing time varies with the weather each year. Call before you go.)

More to See and Do

Fort Toulouse/Jackson Park National Historic Landmark, Wetumpka. Built where the Coosa and Tallapoosa meet, the fort was opened by Bienville in 1717 to establish trade in the heart of Creek territory. Open daily from 6 a.m. to 9 p.m. except for January 1, December 25 and Thanksgiving Day. Admission is $1 for adults, $.50 for children.

How to Get There

Jasmine Hill Gardens is north of Montgomery off U.S. 231 on Jasmine Hill Road.

Where to Stay

Holiday Inn-East, Montgomery. Indoor pool, putting green, exercise equipment. Non-smoking rooms available.

Fairfield Inn by Marriott. Non-smoking rooms available.

Red Bluff Cottage, Montgomery. A bed and breakfast facility.

Camping is available at Fort Toulouse/Jackson Park National Historic Landmark, Wetumpka.

Where to Eat

Vintage Year, Montgomery. Specializes in seafood, Italian dishes. Restaurant has art gallery. Serves dinner Tuesday through Saturday.

Sassafras Tea Room, Montgomery. Victorian atmosphere sets the stage for dining on home cooking and specialty salads. Serves lunch Monday through Friday.

For More Information

For more information about Jasmine Hill Gardens, call 1-334-263-1440.

Jasmine Hill Garden includes many reproductions of Greek sculpture

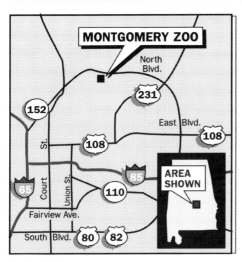

MONTGOMERY, ALABAMA

⊚⊚⊚

Montgomery Zoo

While most people think of going to the zoo as a summer activity, winter may be one of the best times to visit the animals. And Montgomery, with its new zoo expansion and modernization, may well be one of the best places.

The zoo began as a six-acre facility, but has expanded to 40 acres, with new housing for the animals and new ways for visitors to view them.

More than 800 animals from five continents are displayed in barrier-free exhibit areas at the zoo.

The Montgomery Zoo opened at its present location in 1972. "It was very clean and had a nice collection of animals," director Bill Fiore said in a recent Alabama Public Television special about the zoo. But, he added, those animals were displayed behind chain link and bars. It might have been state of the art zoo design at the time, Fiore said, but things have changed.

And the Montgomery Zoo has changed with them. In 1983, the zoo contracted with a zoo planning organization to create a master plan for the facility and the multi-million dollar project was launched. Of course, much of the work at first was planning, done on paper, and fund raising, done in meetings, board rooms and city council meetings.

When the actual work started, though, it really moved along. While many zoos will update or add a display over a span of years, the Montgomery Zoo went from six to 40 acres in less than 12 months.

The zoo has gone from concrete cages to wide open spaces. The new exhibit areas have grass, waterfalls and streams. And animals are displayed in multi-species groups—a big change from the old way of thinking that had one species in each exhibit. The new design has allowed for an expanded collection of animals as well.

The new zoo design may not always make it possible for visitors to walk up to an exhibit "like walking up to a television screen" and immediately spot the animal, said zookeeper Mike Mason. "You may have to work a little to see what you want to see." But the display areas provide the animals a more natural environment, he said.

"You have to walk a fine line between the needs of the animals and the needs of the patrons," he said, " and I think the people who designed the Montgomery Zoo has tried to come up with the best of both worlds."

The zoo is open from 9:30 a.m. to 5:30 p.m. The zoo is closed on Christmas and New Year's. Admission is $4.50 for adults and $1.50 for visitors 4 to 12 years old.

More to See and Do

Civil Rights Memorial. At the corner of Washington Avenue and Hull Street at the Southern Poverty Law Center, the memorial highlights key events of the civil rights struggle and lists the names of more than 30 people who died in the cause of civil rights. There is no charge to view the memorial, which is open to the public 24 hours a day.

Maxwell Air Force Base. On this site, Orville and Wilbur Wright operated one of the world's first flight training schools in 1910. Visitors may drive on base during daylight hours by presenting a valid driver's license. Tours also are available.

How to Get There

Montgomery is in central Alabama on I-65. To get to the zoo, take North Boulevard off I-65 and go east. The entrance to the zoo, at 329 Vandiver Boulevard, is off North Boulevard between the Coliseum and Lower Wetumpka Road exits.

Where to Stay

Courtyard by Marriott. Non-smoking rooms available.

Hampton Inn. Non-smoking rooms available.

Where to Eat

Wesley's. Serves lunch and dinner.

Shashy's Bakery and Fine Foods. 1950s-style diner with deli sandwiches, bakery, hot lunch.

For More Information

For more information about Montgomery, call 1-334-262-0013.

Birds in natural settings can be viewed from elevated walkway at Montgomery Zoo

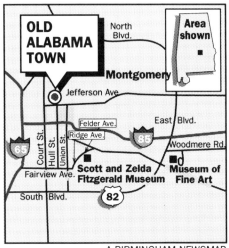

A BIRMINGHAM NEWSMAP

MONTGOMERY, ALABAMA

◉◉◉

Old Alabama Town

On the days that you need a break from computers and telephones, traffic and technology, there is a place where you can escape to a simpler time. Oddly enough, it's in the heart of a city where there's always lots going on— Montgomery.

But Old Alabama Town is Montgomery the way it used to be.

The historic district, set near the State Capitol, brings together several structures that show a little bit of what life was like for the ordinary people who contributed to Alabama's development.

Among the buildings there is Lucas Tavern, a popular stopping place for travelers in the early 1800s. Not all the tavern's patrons were "ordinary folk." Lafayette spent one night as a guest there in the early 1800s.

Also in the district visitors will find a one room log cabin from the early 1800's, a Dogtrot House, and a two-room Shotgun house, typical of the black neighborhoods in the late 1800s.

Other buildings welcoming Old Alabama Town visitors are a grange hall, a barn, a one-room schoolhouse, a corner grocery store, a country doctor's office and a church that housed a black Presbyterian congregation.

The most pretentious structure in the district is the Ordeman-Shaw House, an Italianate residence built in 1848.

The buildings in the district are furnished with period pieces and costumed guides talk about what living was like in Alabama in the 1800s.

The district is open daily, except for January 1, Thanksgiving and Christmas. Hours are 9:30 a.m. to 3:30 p.m., Monday through Saturday and 1:30 to 3:30 p.m. on Sunday. Admission is $5., $2 6-18. This admission includes a guide tape to explain things visitors see as they make their way through the district.

More to See and Do

Montgomery Museum of Fine Arts. The museum is set in the Wynton Blount Cultural Park, where the buildings surround a lake, and houses the Blount collection of paintings as well as collections of European art and regional and decorative arts. A portion of the museum is devoted to a children's hands-on art area. The museum is open from 10 a.m. to 5 p.m. Tuesday, Wednesday, Friday and Saturday and from 10 a.m. to 9 a.m. on Thursday. Sunday hours are noon to 5 p.m. Admission is free.

How to Get There

Montgomery is in central Alabama on I-65.

Where to Stay

Best Western Peddler's Inn. Non-smoking rooms available.

Red Bluff Cottage. A bed and breakfast inn.

Where to Eat

Martha's Place, 431 Sayre St. There's usually a line at the door of the two-story clapboard house on the predominantly black Sayre Street. In the line, there's likely to be businessmen, tourists and politicians. Food here is cooked the Southern way with fresh ingredients. Martha's Place is open for lunch from 11 a.m. to 3 p.m.

The Young House. Located in Old Alabama Town, this restaurant serves lunch only.

For More Information

For more information about Old Alabama Town, call 1-334-240-4500. For more information about Montgomery, call the Visitor Information Center (located in the historic district near Old Alabama Town), 1-334-262-0013.

A BIRMINGHAM NEWSMAP

MOORESVILLE, ALABAMA

In 1818, even before there was a state of Alabama, there was a Mooresville. Now, more than 150 years later, Mooresville still is there and the entire town remains much the same as it was when it was incorporated.

The streets and lots in the small north Alabama community are the same ones that were laid out when the town came into being. Even though Mooresville isn't that far from bustling, growing cities, the town has let time pass it by like the busy traffic on interstates that run nearby.

Among the early residents of Mooresville was Joseph Sloss, an Irish immigrant who set up a tailor shop in Mooresville in 1819. Young men from all over the country came to be apprenticed to Sloss, working with him in what now is known as the Thatch-Hurn-Boozer-McNeal Home. Andrew Johnson, who left the tailoring business and became the nation's 17th president, was one of those apprentices. The home where he worked with Sloss still stands.

Johnson wasn't the only future president who is said to have spent time in Mooresville. General James Garfield, it is said, preached at the Church of Christ there during the Civil War.

William McKinley also is said to have preached in the church, where Garfield's Bible is on display.

Another church the old Brick Church, is set on property donated by Alabama's second governor Thomas Bibb and his wife

Pamela. The Bibbs, who had a summer home in nearby Belle Mina, specified that the land be used for a community church.

It is easy to see Mooresville in just a day, even if you take a leisurely, 19th-century paced walk along the streets, shaded by oaks planted by the town's original settlers.

To help you find your way around, you can stop at the post office and get a copy of "A Walking Tour of Mooresville."

How to Get There

Mooresville is located on Highway 71, south of I-565 between Decatur and Huntsville.

Where to Stay

Amberley Suite Hotel, Decatur. All-suite facility. Non-smoking rooms available.

Days Inn, Decatur. Non-smoking rooms available.

Holiday Inn, Decatur. Non-smoking rooms available.

Camping is available at Point Mallard, Decatur.

Where to Eat

Court Street Cafe, Decatur. Serves lunch and dinner daily.

McCollum's Seafood Restaurant, Decatur. Open from 8 a.m. to 9 p.m. Tuesday through Saturday.

Big Bob Gibson's Bar-B-Q. Open daily from 9 a.m. to 8:30 p.m.

For More Information

For more information about Mooresville, call the Alabama Mountain Lakes Tourist Association, 1-800-648-5381.

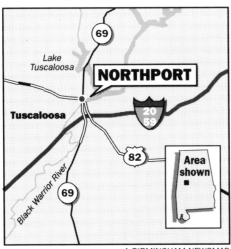

A BIRMINGHAM NEWSMAP

NORTHPORT, ALABAMA

◉◉◉

Kentuck Museum

At first, it may seem a little surprising to find an art colony perched on Main in a small Alabama town—sort of a throwback to the "artsy" age of the 60's. Once you start visiting with the artists, though, it begins to seem very natural—and very 90's—to find these people working in Northport.

The art colony—Kentuck Art Center—gets its name from the first name given to Northport. Originally called Kentuck, the city was the site of an early ford used by travelers crossing the Black Warrior River as they made their way across the Alabama Territory. When a community sprang up at the river crossing, it seemed natural to name it Northport—a port on the north side of the river.

The center houses the studios of professional, full-time artists in three of Northport's early 20th-century shops (including the city's first service station). The artists who work there have become an important part of Northport's past and future as they create contemporary art pieces in historic buildings.

Craig Nutt, a woodworker who crafts whimsical furniture as well as sculpture, does his work in the back corner studio. Other artists who work at the Center include musical instrument maker Anden Houben and Steven Davis, photographer.

The Kentuck Museum, located in Northport Civic Center, gives not only these artists, but many others the opportunity to introduce the public to their latest works. The museum features changing exhibits of traditional craft and contemporary art.

Museum hours are 9 a.m. to 5 p.m. Monday through Friday and 10 a.m. to 2 p.m. Saturday. Artists welcome visitors to their studios in the Art Center, but do not always keep regular hours. A call to the Museum will tell you when artists will be available.

More to See and Do

North River Historical Area. Several Alabama landmarks have been relocated here and restored by the Gulf State Paper Corporation. Among the buildings on the site are Old Center Church (1870), Umbria Schoolhouse (1820), The Gainesville Bank (1835) and a dogtrot cabin from 1837.

How to Get There

Northport is on U.S. 82 northwest of Tuscaloosa.

Where to Stay

Sheraton Capstone, Tuscaloosa. Non-smoking rooms available.

Holiday Inn, Tuscaloosa. Non-smoking rooms available.

Ramada Inn, Tuscaloosa. Non-smoking rooms available.

Camping is available at Deerlick Creek Campground.

Where to Eat

Globe Restaurant. The Globe has a deli type atmosphere with a much larger menu, featuring gourmet cuisine from around the world.

Archibald's Barbecue. Several "locals" say this is a must for barbecue connoisseurs.

Heritage House Coffee Shop. The shop features a full line of gourmet coffees to enjoy with the cheesecake and fresh pastries.

For More Information

For more information about Kentuck Museum and Northport, call 1-205-333-1252.

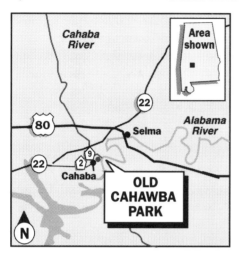

SELMA, ALABAMA

◉◉◉

Old Cahawba

When Alabama became a state in 1819, the city of Cahawba, on a bluff overlooking the confluence of the Alabama and Cahaba Rivers was created by William Wyatt Bibb to be the first permanent state capital. The new town also became the seat of Dallas County.

A copper-domed State House was built and a building boom swept the city. Houses, state buildings and churches went up. Steamboats arrived regularly with Parisian furnishings, chandeliers, china and fabrics.

The city also found itself the social center of the state. Historians record that the dinners were more bountiful, the horses better groomed, the voices more gentle in this city than anywhere else in the state.

So lavish was the partying here, in fact, that the town almost broke the state bank when, in 1825, a party was given for General Marquis de Lafayette, the French hero of the Revolutionary War.

A fatal blow struck Cahawba as the state capital the next year when a flood swept down the rivers and into the city. The state capital was moved to Tuscaloosa.

Cahawba remained the county seat, however, until two more events sounded the end of the city forever. The Civil War took most of the men from the city and another flood, this one even worse than the one before it, left the city in ruins.

54

Cahawba lost its place as the county seat—as well as many of its citizens—to Selma. The buildings of Cahawba were razed so materials could be used to build homes in other cities. Many of the homes of Selma were made from the brick, board and glass of Cahawba.

The copper dome from the State House was moved to the Lowndesboro CME Church.

Visitors to Cahawba today make their way down a country road off Alabama 22 south of Selma. The city's streets still can be traced, though some of them end in a mass of trees and others at the banks of the Alabama River.

Markers designate the location of some of the buildings in Cahawba and the remains of some others still are visible.

The location of a city that once hosted Lafayette now is Old Cahawba State Park, with trails through the area to guide visitors into the city's past and a Welcome Center with displays and information on the history of the area. The park is open daily from 9 a.m. to 5 p.m.

More to See and Do

Sturdivant Hall and Museum, Selma. One of the South's outstanding Greek Revival antebellum homes. Tour includes the house, detached kitchen and formal garden. Open 9 a.m. to 4 p.m. Tuesday through Saturday. and 2 to 4 p.m. Sunday. Admission is $5 for adults and $2 for students. Children under six are admitted free.

Old Depot Museum, Selma. Traces the area's history from the Civil War to Civil Rights. Hours are 10 a.m. to 4 p.m. Monday through Saturday and 2 to 5 p.m. Sunday. Admission is $4 for adults and $1 for students.

National Voting Rights Museum and Institute, Selma. Open Tuesday through Friday, 1 to 5 p.m. and Saturday, 10 a.m. to 5 p.m. Admission is $4 for adults and $2 for children.

How to Get There
Old Cahawba Park is 13 miles west of Selma on County Road 9.

Where to Stay
Jameson Inn, Selma.

Best Western Hotel, Selma.

Grace Hall, Selma. A bed and breakfast facility. Non-smoking rooms available.

Camping is available at Paul M. Grist State Park and Roland Cooper State Park.

Where to Eat
Tally-Ho, Selma.

Hancock's Bar-B-Que, Selma.

For More Information
For more information about Selma and Old Cahawba, call 1-800-628-4291.

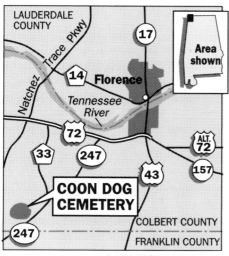

A BIRMINGHAM NEWSMAP

TUSCUMBIA, ALABAMA

⊙⊙⊙

The setting is serene. The sound effects are provided by birds and other creatures. The landscape is dotted with trees, flowers and tombstones—from elaborate marble monuments to simple wooden markers. It is, one realizes quickly, the perfect place to lay a dear friend to rest.

That's what more than 100 humans have done for canine friends with whom they've formed that bond that can only be understood by another human and his dog.

It has been almost 60 years since Key Underwood brought his coon dog Troop to this spot where they often had hunted together, dug a grave and buried his friend beneath the familiar ground. Although Underwood had not intended to start a tradition—or a cemetery for that matter—he did. Owners of "tried and true" coon dogs have buried their dogs here (Coon dogs are the only ones allowed in the cemetery.), marked their graves and, often, visit them regularly to decorate the graves and talk about their dogs.

Surprisingly, Troop's grave bears one of the simpler markers, with little more information than his name. "Doctor Doom's" grave is marked with a marble monument outlining his championship wins and bearing a carving of a coon dog treeing a raccoon.

"The Best East of the Mississippi River" proclaims the marker on the grave of "Bragg," owned by Bill McCorkle of Florence.

Another marker says that "Rusty," who died May 22, 1981, was "A Coon Dog Indeed."

While the cemetery and its surrounding park is quiet most of the year, there is one time when the park takes precedence over the cemetery. On Labor Day each year, a celebration—with music from bluegrass music to dancing—is held at the cemetery. In a tribute to the fact that men who hunt may rank right up there with men who fish when it comes to stretching the truth about "the one that got away," there is a Liar's Contest at the celebration. And there is southern barbecue to keep the celebrants going.

To reach the Key Underwood Coon Dog cemetery, drive about seven miles west of Tuscumbia on U.S. 72 West and turn left on Alabama 247. Go about 12 miles, turn right and follow the signs to the cemetery.

More to see and do:

Wilson Lock and Dam, Florence. The lock and dam complex began as a World War I munitions project. Today, it's one of those tourist attractions that people don't really figure they'd go to see, but keep coming back to once they've seen it. Among the engineering feats on display is one of the world's highest single-lift locks.

How to get there

Tuscumbia is in northwestern Alabama just off Alternate U.S. 72, about 70 miles northwest of Cullman.

Where to stay

Key West Inn, Tuscumbia. Free Continental breakfast. Non-smoking rooms available.

Wood Avenue Inn, Florence. A bed and breakfast.

The Cypress Inn, Florence. A bed and breakfast.

Camping is available at Cherokee Overnight RV Park and Colbert County Park.

Where to eat

Southland, Sheffield.

Southern Diner. Serves lunch and dinner Tuesday through Sunday.

Sid's. This restaurant is part deli, part '50s ice-cream parlor. You'll find the menus on the tables, literally. That's where they are printed. One of the most popular items is the Susie-Q Special, a sandwich of ham, turkey and two cheeses. It's also a great place to get an old-fashioned banana split. Serves lunch daily.

For more information

For more information about Tuscumbia, call 1-205-383-0783.

AREA SHOWN

A BIRMINGHAM NEWSMAP

AMELIA ISLAND, FLORIDA

◉◉◉

Amelia Island, sitting just off the northeast coast of Florida, seems to lean heavily toward its English ancestry. But the island, with its sparkling beaches, has belonged to many governments in her four century long history.

Named for the unmarried daughter of King George II, Amelia has is a barrier island and, for the most part, is less developed and less commercial than some of the others. It has only one incorporated city— Fernandina Beach. In that town's name, another part of the island's history is told. The city is named for King Ferdinand VII of Spain.

The French claimed the island in 1582 and the Spanish were the next to own it. The Patriots flag flew over the island in 1812 and then a quick succession of flags—General Sir Gregor MacGregor's personal flag, the Green Cross of Florida and the flag of Mexico—flew there.

The United States took possession of the island in 1821 and raised the U.S. flag. It was replaced by the Confederate flag that flew over Fort Clinch and Fernandina during the early part of the Civil War. That flag came down in 1862, when the town was the target of a Union fleet.

Today, Amelia Island salutes her heritage at the Amelia Island Museum of History. The museum houses artifacts from digs at a Spanish mission site and from each flag period from 1562 to the

19th century.

Docents at the museum give visitors a guided tour (making it one of the few oral history museums around) and guides also offer a walking tour of Fernandina Beach's Historic District. Walking tours of the museum are given at 11 a.m and 2 p.m. daily except Sunday.

More to See and Do

Centre Street, Fernandina Beach. Located in Fernandina Beach's 50-block Historic District, this shopping district is made up of renovated buildings that now house boutiques in their 19th-century walls. Victorian homes line the side streets.

Amelia Island Lighthouse. The 1839 lighthouse is among the oldest structures on the island. Its beacon can be seen 19 miles out to sea.

Sea Horse Stables. If your idea of romance involves you and your loved one riding sleek steeds down a deserted beach, then check out the rates at the stables. Romantic dreams sometimes can come true.

How to Get There

Amelia Island is located northeast of Jacksonville, Fla., on Florida A1A.

Where to Stay

Amelia Island Plantation. This one has it all—indoor/outdoor pools, a boardwalk through a sunken garden, golf courses, beaches and bike trails, just to name a few. Non-smoking rooms available.

Shoney's Inn, Fernandina Beach.

The 1735 House, Amelia Island. On the beach, the inn is set in a 1928 building and named for the year the island was discovered.

The Bailey House Inn, Fernandina Beach. An 1895 Queen Ann-style house with turrets and gables. Non-smoking.

The Phoenix Nest, Fernandina Beach. The inn is set in a 1938 beach house.

Camping is available at Fort Clinch State Park.

Where to Eat

The Coop. Locals say this is a great place for a family breakfast or lunch. Open daily from 8 a.m. to 3 p.m.

Florida House Inn. Real Southern cooking served boarding house style. Serves lunch Monday through Saturday, lunch and dinner Tuesday through Saturday and Sunday brunch.

Maggie's Diner, Fernandina Beach. A trip back to the 50's. Serves breakfast and lunch as well as Sunday brunch.

For More Information

For more information about Amelia Island, call the Amelia Island/Fernandina Beach/Yulee Chamber of Commerce, 1-800-226-3542.

PANAMA CITY, FLORIDA

◉◉◉

Winter at the Beach

While most people think of the beach as a summer destination, the late fall and early winter can be among the nicest times to make the trip to the Florida coast.

In the Panama City area, this is the off-season-rates are down and it's less crowded than during the summer.

And just about the only things you'll be missing out on by going during this season are few of the attractions geared to the younger crowd—go-cart tracks, the water parks, miniature golf and the amusement park. But the locals say you "still can find an airbrushed T-shirt during this time if you can't go home without one."

There still are trips to Shell Island and the water temperatures are nice and warm even if the days are a little cooler than in the summer. In fact, the water may be nicer than you remember it during your last summer trip. Seaweed isn't as prevalent during the fall and winter and the water now may be the clearest of all.

The sunsets and sunrises stay just as magnificent during this season and walks on the beach usually don't require a lot of bundling up since the weather generally is mild.

The beach in the winter is a great, inexpensive getaway and who knows what new things you might find to like about the beach if you aren't spending all your time wondering whether the side with the dinosaur and the volcano or the side with the pirate ship and the treasure cave is the easier miniature golf course?

More to See and Do

Junior Museum of Bay County. Venture into Panama City itself and discover something that may not have occurred to you before. People live in this area all year long and have museums and the like the same way everyone else does.

This happens to be a very nice museum for the younger crowd. On the grounds, you'll find a reconstructed log cabin, a grist mill and a cane mill. Exhibits inside include some hands-on experiments for the youngsters as well as permanent and changing displays for all ages. A nature trail takes visitors on an elevated walkway through a hardwood swamp and a pine island. The museum is open from 9 a.m. to 4 p.m. Tuesday through Saturday and from 1 to 4 p.m. Sunday. Admission is free.

How to Get There

Panama City Beach is located in the Florida Panhandle on U.S. 98.

Where to Stay

Marriott's Bay Point Resort, Panama City. Five swimming pools, a golf course, a marina, tennis courts, exercise rooms and numerous restaurants make this a sort of "lap of luxury" getaway spot for the winter traveler. Non-smoking rooms available.

Holiday Inn, Panama City Beach. Non-smoking rooms available.

Best Western Bayside Inn, Panama City.

One word: If you have a favorite place to stay in Panama City or Panama City Beach, check to be sure it's open before you head down. Most of the larger facilities are open year round, but you will find some of the others closed during the winter.

Where to Eat:

Montego Bay Restaurants, Panama City Beach. Four locations, specializing in seafood.

Hamilton's, Panama City Beach. Continental menu specializing in seafood, pasta and mesquite-grilled dishes. Victorian decor, overlooking lagoon. Serves dinner.

Note: Some of the restaurants in the area close for at least part of the winter. Captain Anderson's, for example, closes at the end of October. If you've got your tastebuds all set for a certain meal, check before you go.

For More Information:

For more information about Panama City Beach, call the Information Center, 1-800-PC-BEACH (1-800-722-3224).

Winter days are often balmy and beaches uncrowded along the northern Gulf coast

GEORGIA

Buena
Vista

26 Ellaville 49

228

Andersonville

153

Andersonville
Historic Site

27 Americus

45 Plains 280

Leslie

49

19

Montezuma

90

Flint River

A BIRMINGHAM NEWSMAP

ANDERSONVILLE, GEORGIA

◉◉◉

Today, the visitor to the Andersonville National Historic Site in Georgia walks among calm, serene oaks and magnolias on a blanket of green grass.

The place wasn't always a place of peace. Andersonville was the site of the largest of the Confederate military prisons, built in 1863 by soldiers and slaves gathered from the nearby plantations. Built to accommodate 10,000 men, it frequently held more than 30,000 during its 14 months of existence.

The prisoners who were unfortunate enough to be sent to Andersonville suffered from lack of food, disease, overcrowding and exposure.

Trenches three feet deep served as burial sites for the almost 13,000 Union soldiers and sailors who died there. The graves are all that remain of the prison.

All of the buildings were torn down after the war ended. The place where it once stood now is the Andersonville National Historic Site, a memorial to all the prisoners of war throughout history.

On the site, visitors can see escape tunnels and wells dug by prisoners. Also on the site is a reconstructed section of stockade wall and Confederate earthworks. Many states have erected monuments to their soldiers who died in Andersonville.

A Visitors Center provides background information about the

site and several listings of prisoners held there. Andersonville also is the site of the nation's first Prisoner of War museum.

Visitors at first may be taken aback by some of the newer headstones in the Andersonville cemetery. The Union dead are not the only ones buried there. Federal law allows any veteran—and his spouse—to be buried in Andersonville and many of them, after visiting the site, have chosen it as their burial site.

More to See and Do

Confederate Village. Located across from the prison, the restored village includes a log church (built in 1927 and designed by the same people who did the Cathedral of St. John the Divine in New York City), prison officials' quarters, a pioneer farm and a museum. Open seven days a week. Admission is free.

Lindbergh Memorial, Americus. Charles Lindbergh purchased his first plane in Americus and made his first solo flight here in 1923. The plane, sold as World War I government surplus, cost Lindbergh $500. The memorial commemorates Lindbergh's visit to the city.

How to Get There

Andersonville is southeast of Columbus on Georgia 49.

Where to Stay

Windsor Hotel, Americus. Century-old building recently renovated. One of the two hotels in Georgia on the National Trust for Historic Preservation.

The Cottage Inn, Americus. A bed and breakfast facility.

A Place Away, Andersonville. A bed and breakfast facility.

Camping is available at Andersonville RV Park.

Where to Eat

Daphne Lodge, Cordele. Set in Plantation manor house. Specialties are catfish, seafood and steak. Serves dinner only. Closed Sunday and Monday.

Olde Inn, Cordele. Set in building from the late 1800s. Specialties are seafood, steak. Serves dinner only. Closed Sunday and Monday.

For More Information

For more information about Andersonville, call the Andersonville Welcome Center, 1-912-924-2558.

Row upon row of prisoner of war graves mark the Andersonville site

A BIRMINGHAM NEWSMAP

ATLANTA, GEORGIA

◉◉◉

If you think of Atlanta only as a place with too many Peachtree Streets or somewhere you have to go through to get somewhere else, then you're in for a surprise. Atlanta has some really nice places to visit that only involve getting on one Peachtree Street and aren't just stopovers.

One of them is the Atlanta History Center, a place where the pace is a little slower than in the rest of Atlanta and where you might rediscover a little bit of history.

The History Center sits on 32 acres, filled with gardens, historic homes and even a farm animal or two. Three structures—McElreath Hall, the Swan House and the Tullie Smith House—sit on the property.

McElreath Hall houses two permanent exhibits on the history of Atlanta.

The Swan House is ranked as one of the finest mansions in the South and its grandeur is a testament to the elegant lifestyle enjoyed by its original owners. Outside, the structure is magnificent. Inside, visitors find such treasures as a 1,300-year-old Tang Dynasty terra cotta horse.

The Tullie Smith House, one of the few structures spared by Sherman as he cut his path of destruction through Atlanta, tells of another lifestyle. It's a very back-to-basics building that speaks of a simple, hard-working life.

If you plan to visit the History Center, allow yourself about three hours to see the center and tour the homes there.

The History Center is open from 10 a.m. to 5:30 p.m. Monday through Saturday and from noon to 5:30 p.m. on Sunday. Tours of the homes are given on a timed ticket/first come-first served basis. Tickets must be purchased at least 15 minutes before the tour begins.

Admission to the History Center is $7 for adults, $5 for seniors, $4 for youths. Tours of the homes are $1 per person per home.

More to See and Do

Center for Puppetry Arts. Near the Woodruff Arts Center, this attraction for the young and the young at heart houses the Puppetry of the World Museum. Museum visitors can see one of the largest collections of puppets in the world and learn about the history of puppetry and the art of puppet making. The museum is open 9 a.m.-5 p.m. Monday through Friday. Hours for the workshops and performances vary. Admission is $5.75 for adults and $4.75 for children.

Fox Theater. If you appreciate lovely old movie showplaces, then you've got to at least drive by the Fox. Built in 1929, it recently has been restored and is being used for a number of different kinds of performances. If you are visiting Atlanta during one of these performances, a chance to see the inside of the Fox probably is worth the price of admission. There also are tours of the Fox on Monday, Thursdays and Saturdays at 10 a.m. They cost $5 per person for adults and $3 per person for students and seniors. To join a tour, which lasts about an hour to 90 minutes, call the Atlanta Preservation Society.

How to Get There

The Atlanta History Center is located north of downtown Atlanta off of West Paces Ferry Road at 3101 Andrews Drive NW.

Where to Stay

Colony Square. This 27-story, 500-room hotel is at Peachtree and 14th Street NE.

Westin Peachtree Plaza. One of Atlanta architect John Portman's spectaculars, this is a 73-story structure built in a circular style around an eight-story atrium. The hotel, with almost 1,100 rooms, is at Peachtree and International Boulevard.

The Gaslight Inn. Off Ponce de Leon downtown. A bed and breakfast. It gets its name from the original gaslights still in the structure.

Where to Eat

The Coach House Restaurant. Located in what once were the slave quarters of the Swan House on the grounds of the History Center. Lunch is served there Monday through Saturday.

Coca-Cola Cafe. On the grounds of the History Center. Serves lunch and snacks.

The Varsity. One of the largest drive-in restaurants in the world, The Varsity is on the campus of Georgia Tech. It's a great place for people watching and from some of the seating areas inside the restaurant, you even can watch your food being prepared.

The Buckhead Diner. The specialty of the house is the white chocolate banana cream pie and they also make their own pastries.

For More Information

For more information about the Atlanta History Center, call 1-404-814-4000. For more information about Atlanta, call the Atlanta Convention and Visitors Bureau at 1-404-521-6600.

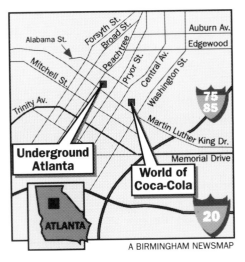

A BIRMINGHAM NEWSMAP

ATLANTA, GEORGIA

◉◉◉

World of Coca-Cola

Perhaps it's one of those things that could happen only in America—a soft drink becomes a tourist attraction. Where else could there be enough to see and say about a bottled mixture of syrup and carbonated water to fill an entire building?

Still, there it is—the World of Coca-Cola—sitting in the heart of downtown Atlanta lighting the landscape with a giant Coca-Cola sign. And there usually are lines outside waiting to get in and see what's there.

Once those people get inside, they find a sort of mixture of shopping mall, refreshment counter, history museum and amusement park.

A tour of the World of Coca-Cola begins with a look at the bottling process and an extensive display of Coke memorabilia.

Among the items on display are the original patent for Coca-Cola, the first calendar used to advertise Coke and examples of advertising featuring celebrities and sports figures who have endorsed the drink throughout the years.

The tour then moves to the third floor, where there are displays saluting Robert Woodruff's contributions to the Coca-Cola empire.

There also is a 1930s-style soda fountain, where a "soda jerk" carries on banter with his "customers" as he shows how Cokes were mixed before and after the invention of modern-day machinery and equipment.

Also on this floor is a juke box with 20 "Coke" songs and 20 excerpts from radio broadcast sponsored by the Coca-Cola Company in the 30s, 40s and 50s.

The second floor of the World of Coca-Cola is where visitors find all the "goodies" to sample. After a look at more displays, they can go to "Club Coca-Cola" to try samples of 18 soft drink flavors found outside the United States. Some of the tastes are more appealing than others—fruit punch from Central America, for example, sounds a lot better than quinine aperitif from Italy.

The final area in "Club Coca-Cola" features a spectacular soda fountain that allows visitors to sample various Coca-Cola products. To have a taste of the beverage of choice, one fills a glass with ice, steps up to the brand he has chosen and watches as the liquid streams 20 feet through the air before coming to rest in the cup.

To achieve the effect, the builders and designers installed more than 1,000 feet of neon tubing and patented an "ultrasonic level sensor" to determine how much liquid it will take to fill each cup.

More than 1 million visitors have sipped and sampled their way through the building since it opened in August, 1990, and it seems—like the Coca-Cola products and the "singable" Coke jingles—they will keep on coming.

The World of Coca-Cola is open from 10 a.m. to 8:30 p.m. Monday through Saturday and from noon to 5 p.m. on Sunday. It is closed New Year's Day, Easter, Thanksgiving, Christmas Eve and Christmas Day. Admission is $3.50 for adults, $3 for seniors (55 and over) and $2.50 for children 6 to 12 years old.

More to See and Do

Atlanta Botanical Garden. Outdoor gardens spread across this 15-acre complex. There also is an herb garden and the Fuqua Conservatory, which features rare plants from all over the world and a special area for carnivorous plants. Hours are 9 a.m.-7 p.m. Tuesday through Sunday, and admission is $6. for adults, $5 for seniors and $3 for students and children.

73

How to Get There

The World of Coca-Cola is located in downtown Atlanta at 55 Martin Luther King Jr. Drive (at Central Avenue). It is across from the Kenny's Alley entrance to Underground Atlanta.

Where to Stay

The Westin Peachtree. Non-smoking rooms available.

The Beverly Hills Inn. A bed and breakfast.

Camping is available in Stone Mountain Park.

Where to Eat

Pano's and Paul's. This one is an award winner, so expect a rather hefty check if you decide to go here. Reservations are accepted and recommended. Jackets are required.

City Grill. Another award-winning restaurant. Jackets are required at dinner.

For More Information

For more information about the World of Coke, call 1-404-676-5151. For more information about Atlanta, call the Atlanta Convention and Visitors Bureau at 1-404-521-6600.

A BIRMINGHAM NEWSMAP

BRASELTON, GEORGIA

◉◉◉

Chateau Elan

The 16th century-style French chateau rises above the countryside, surrounded by vineyards that produce the grapes used to make award winning wines. It wouldn't be an unusual sight in France. It does look a little different perched on a hilltop near Braselton, Georgia.

So just how did a French chateau/winery/"mini-resort" end up in Georgia? Donald E. Panoz, founder of Chateau Elan, was visiting Georgia from Ireland in 1981 when he noticed native American vineyards along the rural roads. Why not create vineyards and a winery—and maybe a resort-type recreation center—here? It didn't really matter to him that Georgia wasn't exactly a traditional wine producing state.

"I like the challenge of doing something nobody else is doing," Panoz told those who asked about his decision. It's probably safe to say that not many others are growing more than 200 acres of several varieties of grapes in Georgia and turning them into wines that have won more than 167 medals.

And what about the "recreation center" Panoz planned? Today, the chateau has two restaurants, shopping areas and wine-tasting areas in a setting reminiscent of Paris in the early 1930s. Outside the chateau, visitors will find a sheltered area that hosts summer concerts and a dance floor.

The resort also has a championship golf course, residential

country estates, nature trails, an equestrian trail and picnic areas.

Also on the grounds is a European style health spa, which offers full spa services and personalized wellness programs. The spa also houses 14 guest rooms, each designed with a different decor.

Chateau Elan, about 30 minutes north of Atlanta, opens at 10 a.m. every day. Admission is free. Tours of the winery are given every hour from noon to 5 p.m. Visitors also may try the Chateau Elan wines at wine tastings throughout the day.

More to See and Do

Fort Yargo State Park, Winder. In addition to having the usual camping and picnicking facilities found at most state parks, Fort Yargo also has Will-A-Way Recreational Area. Will-A-Way is designed to be convenient for handicapped persons. A nature trail winds through the area.

How to Get There

Chateau Elan is northeast of Atlanta, off I-85 at Exit 48.

Where to Stay

Chateau Elan Spa. The European-style spa on the grounds is super-luxurious, with prices to match.

Petite Chateau Villas, Chateau Elan Gold Club. Each villa has a fireplace, patio and fully equipped kitchen.

Camping is available at Fort Yargo State Park.

Where to Eat

There are several restaurants on the Chateau Elan property, featuring everything from gourmet foods, chosen to match the winery's products to Southern dishes.

For More Information

For more information about Chateau Elan, call 1-800-233-WINE.

CAVE SPRING, GEORGIA

◉ ◉ ◉

There was a time when visitors flocked to Cave Spring, Georgia, for its water. Today, the water still attracts some, but you'll probably find more people in town shopping for antiques than for something pure to drink.

The small northwest Georgia city is located in Vann's Valley, named for a Cherokee Indian Chief who died just before his tribe was forced to leave the valley in 1838. The Cherokees were the first to discover the natural wonders the area had to offer.

And the Indians weren't the only ones who found out about Cave Spring. The first settlers, who took land grants from the state, began arriving in Vann's Valley in the 1820s. And before long, many Georgia citizens were arriving in Cave Spring to "take the cure"— enjoy the health benefits of the mineral springs.

Old family correspondences tell of friends or relatives who had been to the city for treatments at the popular spa.

But the history of Cave Spring goes back beyond the white man and the Indian. More than 300,000 years ago, a natural limestone cave with an underground lake began to be created. The cave—and the spring that comes from its lake—gave the city its name.

In addition to providing bottled water for residents and visitors to drink, the spring also flows out to a reflection pond and shallow stream, perfect for little ones to wade in. It then goes on to fill a 1.5-acre swimming pool where bathers can enjoy the mineral waters.

The pool, a number of historic buildings and the cave—open daily for tours from Memorial Day to Labor Day and by appointment at other times—all are part of Rolater Park, in the heart of downtown Cave Spring.

In fact, there are more than 90 historic buildings and sites in the city.

A town of less than 1,000 people with only one traffic light, Cave Spring has held tightly to its past. There are Gothic, Victorian and Plantation style homes, churches and 19th century hotels and boarding houses.

These structures now are enjoying a second life as stores, shops, restaurants and art studios.

Antique hunters can find plenty of shops to explore on a visit to Cave Spring. The shops have everything from furniture to glassware and jewelry to linens. Other stores have folk art, memorabilia and gifts.

Cave Spring also has a thriving art and craft community, producing pottery, bronze art, paintings, furniture, carousel horses and porcelains.

More to See and Do

Cave Spring Baptist Church. Built in 1851, the building is constructed of handmade brick. The balcony, built for the slave members of the church, has a hand-turned rail. The building has its original wide plank floors and stained glass windows.

Fannin Hall. The first permanent building of the Georgia School for the Deaf, which is located in Cave Spring, was built in 1848. It was closed during the Civil War and was used as a hospital for forces on both sides.

Chubbtown Methodist Church. Chubbtown, just east of Cave Spring, was settled in the mid-1800s. It was one of the few communities of free blacks in pre-Civil War Georgia. Chubbtown once had a gin, a grist mill, a general store, a syrup mill, a post office, a distillery, a blacksmith shop and a casket company. The town prospered until about 1920, when much of the city was destroyed by a flood. The church building is the only original structure still standing in Chubbtown. The original pews still are used there.

How to Get There

Cave Spring is in northwest Georgia, about 15 miles southwest of Rome on U.S. 411.

Where to Stay

Hearn Academy Inn. Bed and breakfast in the heart of town. Set in building that once served as a dormitory for a boys' prep school established by the Baptist Church.

Cedar Creek Chalets.

Where to Eat

Shumate's Diner. Serves breakfast and lunch.

Todd's Country Kitchen. Serves lunch and dinner.

Martha Jane's Fudge. Open 10 a.m. to 6 p.m.

Cave Spring Ice Cream Shop. Serves a variety of ice creams as well as items from a short-order kitchen. Serves lunch and dinner.

For more information

For more information about Cave Spring, call 1-706-777-3382.

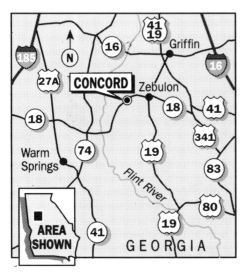

CONCORD, GEORGIA

◉◉◉

Inn Scarlett's Footsteps

When K.C. Bassham was a little girl growing up in Ohio, she went to see "Gone With the Wind." As she sat watching the movie, she vowed to herself that someday she would have a house like the magnificent Wilkes' home, Twelve Oaks.

Today, she's living out that dream in a bed and breakfast set in an 8,000-square foot mansion in Concord, Georgia. The house also is home to Mrs. Bassham's ever growing collection of GWTW memorabilia.

"Some people just don't get it," Mrs. Bassham laughed as she remembered some of the people who have interviewed her since she and her husband Vern bought the house in 1992. "I had one woman tell me I was crazy. I said, 'Good crazy or bad crazy?' She said, 'Good crazy, but you're crazy.' I told her it was okay as long as it was good crazy."

Many of the guests at her inn come there because they, too, have a little bit of the "crazies" for the movie that premiered in 1939. And they are treated to Southern hospitality mixed with a touch of the spice that made Scarlett's America's darling.

Each of her guest rooms has a name and a theme to match. Mr. Gerald's room is reminiscent of Mr. O'Hara's equestrian interests. Ashley's room has a military flair. Melanie's room, naturally, is feminine and refined.

Rhett's room, the second most requested, has an air of masculine sophistication. Scarlett's room, the one most of the guests ask for, is done in strong vibrant colors, with a touch of magnolias thrown in for good measure.

Outside, there are towering trees and even a few horses to add to the authenticity of the GWTW look.

A stay at the inn includes a tour of part of Mrs. Bassham's museum collection, which also is open for public tours. But the collection, like the popularity of GWTW, has just kept growing over the years.

Since it more than fills the museum room at the house, much of it now occupies a museum in nearby Warm Springs.

Rates for an evening with Scarlett, Rhett and their friends the Basshams range from $69 to $79, which includes a full Southern breakfast.

More to See and Do

Last Train to Tara, Warm Springs. When Mrs. Bassham's "Gone With the Wind" collection had more than outgrown the museum room at Inn Scarlett's Footsteps, the Basshams opened this museum in a train car parked in nearby Warm Springs. The museum is open from 11 a.m. to 5 p.m. Tuesday through Saturday and from noon to 5 p.m. Sunday. Admission is $3 for adults, $2.50 for senior citizens and $1 for children.

How to Get There

Don't just rely on looking at a map to find Concord, Georgia. There are at least three cities with that name. The correct Concord is northeast of Warm Springs on Georgia 18.

To reach Inn Scarlett's Footsteps, continue on Georgia 18 through Concord about four-tenths of a mile past the R.F. Strickland Building. The sign is on the right.

Where to Stay

If Inn Scarlett's Footsteps is full, but you'd still like to tour the home or visit the museum, try:

Hotel Warm Springs, Warm Springs. A bed and breakfast facility.

Holiday Inn, Griffin.

Camping is available at Roosevelt State Park, near Pine Mountain.

Where to Eat
Manhattan's Restaurant, Griffin. Fine dining. Serves lunch and dinner.

Jasmine at Dovedown, Griffin. Set in an old hosiery mill. Serves sandwiches, soups and quiche at lunch. Steaks and chicken are dinner specialties.

For More Information
For more information about Inn Scarlett's Footsteps, call 1-706-495-9012.

Inn Scarlett's Footsteps, where Gone With The Wind *lives*

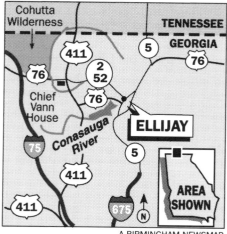

A BIRMINGHAM NEWSMAP

ELLIJAY, GEORGIA

◉◉◉

There are certain sights and sounds that just go with fall—brightly colored leaves that crunch underfoot signal the changing of the season each year. If fall has a taste, it surely must be crisp apples, freshly picked and shiny in greens, yellows and reds.

Fall is the perfect time to explore the apple houses of North Georgia. Finding apples in abundance is no problem. The hard part is deciding which ones to get.

The heart of apple country in North Georgia has to be the town of Ellijay in Gilmer County, where 60 percent of the state's apple trees are found. The trees there produce about 400,000 bushels of apples each year.

From late August to December, the roadside stands (or apple houses) of the county, nestled in the Appalachians, are filled with apples from Gala and Red and Golden Delicious, available early, to Stayman Winesaps, Arkansas Blacks and Granny Smiths, which ripen late in the season.

An additional payoff for those who make the trip to buy their own apples direct from the growers is that the mountains nearby are filled with fall colors during apple season.

Some apple hunting tips:

1. Call ahead and get a map to the various apple house locations.

2. Get to the area early enough to visit all the stops, compare types and prices and make a decision on what you want to buy.

3. Go prepared to find more than just apples. The locations usually have apple butter and other jellies and jams, honey, apple breads, apple pies and, depending on the season, pumpkins, nuts, fall squash and Indian corn.

4. Decide if you want to pick your own. Some of the growers have "pick your own" apples. If you want to do this, you need to go dressed for apple picking.

More to See and Do:

Chief Vann House, Chatsworth. The multi-storied brick mansion, built in the early 1800s by James Vann, was one of the first of its kind in Cherokee country. Vann, half Scottish and half Cherokee, helped establish the nearby Moravian Mission for the education of young Cherokees. When Vann died, his son Joseph inherited the property and lived there until 1834, when he was evicted shortly before the Trail of Tears movement began. The house museum is open from 9 a.m. to 5 p.m. Tuesday through Saturday and from 2 to 5:30 p.m. Sunday. Admission is $2 for adults and $1 for children.

How to Get There

Ellijay is located in north Georgia southeast of Dalton on U.S. Highway 76.

Where to Stay

Top O'Ellijay/Budget Host Inn. Non-smoking rooms available.

Elderberry Inn, Ellijay. A bed and breakfast facility.

Camping is available at Fort Mountain State Park.

Where to Eat

The Happy Family 2. Chinese cuisine. Serves lunch and dinner daily.

Riverstreet Cafe. A favorite of locals. Serves lunch Monday through Saturday.

Poole's Real Pit Bbq. Serves lunch Monday through Saturday.

For More Information

For more information about Ellijay, call the Gilmer County Chamber of Commerce, 1-706-635-7400.

Apples and crafts highlight a visit to Ellijay

LOOKOUT MOUNTAIN, GEORGIA

⦿⦿⦿

Rock City

A comedian, in a routine about his visit to Nassau (which he called "Nausea"), talks about a trip on a glass bottom boat. The guide told the tourists, according to the comedian, that the body of water on which they were floating was bottomless. "Which bothered me," he says, "because at the time I was looking at the bottom and it said, 'See Rock City'."

If you've ever driven anywhere, you probably have seen the barntops and birdhouses urging you to stop by what has to be Lookout Mountain's most advertised attraction.

And if you've ever been anywhere near Lookout Mountain, you've probably stopped in just to see what all the advertising was about. So you've probably seen Fairyland Caverns, Mother Goose Village and the other rock formations. And you've probably seen the seven states that can be spotted from one vantage point there.

So just how Rock City come to be? It was the brainchild of Garnet Carter, entrepreneur and often professional dreamer. Carter and his partner W.O. Andrews had, in the 1920's, built Fairyland, a luxury home development on Lookout Mountain. When the nation's economy began to suffer, however, so did Fairyland. Garnet had to look for new investments to make.

Carter's wife, Frieda, was the inspiration for his next big ven-

ture—the place   that would become Rock City. The Carters had
bought, along with the acreage for Fairyland, a mountaintop site of
10 acres. Mrs. Carter became intrigued with this mountain acres
and began exploring them.

She laid out the first primitive path through the massive stone
formation. Then she gathered native plants and set them out along
the pathway. Her husband became interested in her efforts and
before long the two of them were working alongside a handful of
assistants to create a tourist attraction they called "Rock City."

Tourist didn't beat a path to the Carters' door until Carter
came up with a unique marketing plan—he would offer to paint
barns along highways free if the owners would allow him to put
three words on the roof: "See Rock City."

Soon the message was everywhere and the invitation seemed
irresistible. Rock City rolled out a welcome mat that still is out
more than 60 years later.

Millions of people have come to follow Frieda Carter's foot-
path through the stone skyscrapers and more than 400,000 still
come annually. New attractions such as Fairyland Caverns, with
fantasy figures and underground lighting, have been added over
the years, but the main attraction still seems to be Mother Nature's
own presentation of peaks and valleys atop the mountain where
the Carters' dream began.

Rock City is open from 8 a.m. to 6:30 p.m. Admission is $8.95
for adults and $4.95 for children.

More to See and Do

Lookout Mountain Incline Railway, Chattanooga. This is one of
the most popular ways to get to the top of Lookout Mountain.
Near the top, the incline of the track is 72.7 degrees, making this
the steepest passenger incline railroad in the world. The Incline
makes three to four trips an hour, beginning at 9 a.m. and ending
at 5:20 p.m. Cost of a round trip is $7 for adults and $4 for children (3-12 years old).

Ruby Falls. A 145-foot waterfall, located in an onyx cave 1,120
feet below the surface of Lookout Mountain, gives this attraction

its name. Ruby Falls is opens each day at 8 a.m. Closing time varies with the season. Cost of a tour of the caverns and falls is $7.50 for adults and $3.50 for children (6 to 12 years old).

How to Get There
Rock City is in the northwest corner of Georgia off Georgia 157. The Lookout Mountain Incline Railway boarding station is at the base of Lookout Mountain in Chattanooga, Tenn., on Tennessee 58. Ruby Falls also is in Chattanooga on Tennessee 148.

Where to Stay
Hampton Inn Lookout Mountain. Free Continental breakfast.

Comfort Inn Lookout Mountain. Some rooms with in-room whirlpools and hot tubs.

Gordon-Lee Mansion. A bed and breakfast near the Chickamauga Battlefield.

Camping is available at KOA Lookout Mountain.

Where to Eat
212 Market Restaurant, Chattanooga.   American cuisine. Serves lunch and dinner daily.

Buck's Bar B Que, Chattanooga. Has been voted Chattanooga's Number One barbecue restaurant. Serves lunch and dinner.

Southern Belle Riverboat, Chattanooga. Often on attractions of this type, the ride is the event and the food is a second thought. Not in this case. On the Southern Belle, the food is an enjoyable as the trip. Lunch and dinner cruises.

For More Information
For more information about Rock City, call 1-706-820-2531. For more information about the Lookout Mountain area, call the Chattanooga, Tenn., Convention and Visitors Bureau at 1-800-322-3344.

A BIRMINGHAM NEWSMAP

PINE MOUNTAIN, GEORGIA

◉◉◉

Callaway Gardens

" Every child ought to see something beautiful before he's six years old— something he will remember all his life." At least that's what Cason J. Callaway believed.

And, because of Callaway and his family, lots of children have seen something beautiful—Callaway Gardens. In fact, more than 750,000 people of all ages come to the Gardens each year.

The land on which the gardens sit "discovered" by Virginia and Cason Callaway on a summer day on 1930. While they were taking a quiet walk through the woods near Pine Mountain, Georgia, the Callaways were taken by the beauty and peacefulness of the area.

They purchased a 2,500-acre tract on which they built a weekend compound. The Callaways eventually owned 40,000 acres, which they carefully managed, planting on hillsides to prevent erosion and working to bring worn-out cotton fields back to life.

In 1948, Cason Callaway suffered a heart attack. After that, he and his wife divided their land among their four children and deeded a fifth portion to the Ida Cason Callaway Foundation, named for his mother.

The Foundation became the new focus of their dreams. They decided to share their surroundings with the public and today's 12,000-acre Callaway Gardens complex is the fulfillment of that plan.

89

Continuously developed over the years, Callaway Gardens now is a year-round recreational area. In the Gardens, there are 2,500 acres of cultivated foliage, walking trails and greenhouses. Visitors also will find facilities for swimming, boating, fishing, cycling, golfing and tennis.

The Gardens' Cecil B. Day Butterfly Center is among the largest glass-enclosed butterfly conservatories in North America.

Each year, the Gardens' visitors come to lose themselves in the resort that was the dream of a man who once said he believed the most interesting ideas are "conceived in superlatives, big in scope, impressive in appearance and in some way connected with the improvement of mankind."

More to See and Do

Pine Mountain Wild Animal Park. Drive your own car or take the Safari Bus through this 500-acre preserve. Admission, in the $10 to $12 range, varies with the season. The park opens at 10 a.m. daily, with closing times changing seasonally.

How to Get There

Callaway Gardens is near Pine Mountain in west Central Georgia. off U.S. 27.

Where to Stay

There are a number of accommodations at Callaway Gardens, including a resort inn, villas and cottages.

Davis Inn, Pine Mountain.

Camping is available at Franklin Roosevelt State Park.

Where to Eat

The Callaway Gardens complex also has a number of restaurants. Among them are the Georgia Room, which serves dinner only (jackets required) and The Country Store, which serves breakfast and lunch in a more casual atmosphere.

McGuire's Family Restaurant, Pine Mountain. Regional eatery featuring catfish and barbecue. Serves breakfast, lunch and dinner daily.

Oak Tree Victorian Restaurant, Pine Mountain. Elegant dining in an 1871 home. Serves dinner.

For More Information

For more information about Callaway Gardens, call 1-800-282-8181.

The flowering trails of Callaway Gardens meander through the Georgia woods

STONE MOUNTAIN

Atlanta

Chattahoochee River

Underground
Atlanta

CNN Center

Jimmy Carter
Library

AREA
SHOWN

STONE MOUNTAIN, GEORGIA

◉◉◉

Stone Mountain Park

As nearly as historians has been able to discover, the first explorer to see Stone Mountain, the huge knot of granite that stands on one of Atlanta's outstretched and ever-growing fingers, was Captain Juan Pardo. Pardo, who came to Georgia in 1567, probably went away wishing he had been able to think of some way to leave his mark on the rock.

Human nature being what it is, it's likely that almost everyone who looked at the mountain in its uncarved state probably would liked to have been the one who did the carving, creating his own little piece of immortality.

It was Gutzon Borglum who originally was chosen to be the creator of a rendering of Robert E. Lee. While Borglum did some work on a carving on the mountain's face, his differences with the project's managers eventually led to his leaving the mountain.

A succession of sculptors and their workmen began to chip away at the granite, carving out images of Jefferson Davis, Lee and Stonewall Jackson astride their horses. Augustus Lukeman started the work in 1925. Work on the carving was halted three years later when the original owners of the land reclaimed their possession.

In 1963, Roy Faulkner and his crew brought a new drilling tool to the mountain and spent six years bringing the figures to life.

In 1970, a formal dedication was held. The three Confederate heroes urged their steeds across a sheer granite background and rode into sculpting history on the largest bas relief sculpture in the world.

The park that has sprung up around the base of the mountain offers visitors more to do than just look at the masterwork of the carvers who created the Stone Mountain Memorial. The park grounds are home to a re-created plantation, a riverboat, a train and a number of museums.

Stone Mountain Park is open daily (Park and attraction hours vary). Admission is $5 for a one-time entry and $20 for an annual pass. There are separate admission charges to some of the attractions at the park. These vary with the attraction.

More to See and Do

Stone Mountain Village. The city that the big rock calls home is worth a visit in itself. The streets in the historic railroad town are lined with quaint shops and eateries.

How to Get There

Stone Mountain is east of Atlanta on U.S. 78.

Where to Stay

Stone Mountain Inn. An inn with a view—of the mountain's face. Non-smoking rooms available.

Evergreen Conference Center and Resort. A part of the complex at Stone Mountain. Non-smoking rooms available.

Camping is available at Stone Mountain Park.

Where to Eat

The Chicken Restaurant. Located at the Stone Mountain Railroad Depot.

Whistle Stop Barbecue. Near the beginning of the walk-up trail at Stone Mountain.

For More Information

For more information about Stone Mountain Park, call 1-404-498-5600.

*Old-time carriage rides are but one
of Stone Mountain's many attractions*

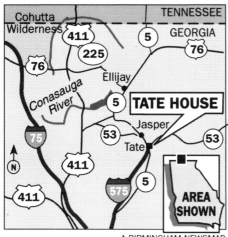

A BIRMINGHAM NEWSMAP

TATE, GEORGIA

◉◉◉

The Tate House

When people discover a hidden treasure, they aren't anxious to share the secret. So it is with the Tate House, tucked away in the mountains of North Georgia.

Those who have discovered the pink marble home don't really like to tell anyone for fear that, before long, everyone will be making this getaway his own.

But it's hard to keep something this good a secret. So here it is. Tate, Ga., literally is a town that marble built.

Many years ago, Samuel Tate discovered a rich vein of marble—2,000 feet wide, four miles long and more than half a mile deep—in the mountains of Georgia. His family mined it for three generations before it was bought out by a large corporation, which now runs one of the nation's largest marble quarry operations there.

Of course, Tate had to build a home in the town where he worked, so in 1926 he constructed a mansion of pink Etowah marble overlooking the Blue Ridge Mountains. And as the town grew, people there began to build all the structures—houses, schools, churches—out of marble. So the entire town has a durable, yet beautiful, look created from the marble upon which it was founded.

Today, Tate's mansion is the Tate House Resort. The house itself has been converted into a bed and breakfast inn with five suites that are furnished with antiques.

The bed and breakfast part of the resort usually is closed during the holidays to make more room for the holiday trappings that decorate the house during this season.

Even when the bed and breakfast is closed, there are nine log cabins, each with the bedroom upstairs and the living room, fireplace and hot tub downstairs.

It's a secret worth finding out about for yourself.

More to See and Do

Amicalola Falls. You can drive to the top and bottom of the falls, Georgia's highest—plunging more than 700 feet in a series of cascades, where there are observation decks.

Amicalola Falls State Park. In addition to the falls, the park offers fishing, camping, hiking and picnicking. For those not inclined to camp out, there are cottages here as well.

The Appalachian National Scenic Trail. The trail, which continues more than 2,000 miles to Mount Katahdin, Maine, begins near Amicalola Falls. The trail follows the crest of the Blue Ridge divide as it makes its way northward. Eleven shelters are maintained along the 80 miles that make up the southern portion of the trail.

How to Get There

Tate is in north central Georgia, about 30 miles northeast of Marietta on Georgia 53.

Where to Stay

Woodbridge Inn, Jasper. Overnight accommodations are provided in a contemporary lodge set next to the inn, which dates from the 1850s. Most of the rooms overlook the Blue Ridge Mountains.

Where to Eat

Woodbridge Inn, Jasper. The owner is from Germany, thus several European dishes appear on the menu here. So many people have found out just how good the food is that reservations are recommended.

For More Information

For more information about the Tate House, call 1-404-735-3122.

North Georgia's Tate House B&B and Resort

A BIRMINGHAM NEWSMAP

WARM SPRINGS, GEORGIA

◉◉◉

Little White House

It probably was the quiet of Warm Springs, Georgia, that appealed to Franklin Roosevelt as much as it was the mineral waters. And miraculously, the years since the president's death haven't taken away the quiet of his retreat.

One still can go there for a respite from the busy world and, even on a day when there are busloads of schoolchildren there, find a quiet place to get away from it all.

A trip to Warm Springs must include a tour of The Little White House—the only home that Franklin Roosevelt ever owned—and a look at the other buildings and memorabilia that still mark the place where the president got away from his office and out among the people.

Seeing the small house, it is hard to imagine that this was a place a President called home, a place to which he made joyful visits, a place he missed when he was away. This man who had the entire Presidential residence to call his own in Washington, D.C., seemed to prefer the cozier confines of this home in rural Georgia.

But it was a different time then. It was a time when Presidents freely drove through town in an open car, waving at passersby and stopping to talk with friends he had made on his previous trips to Warm Springs.

Roosevelt came to take advantage of the healing waters that the town's springs provided. It was a place when his bout with polio didn't make him different, it made him just like everyone else who was there.

And he came to get away from the hustle and bustle of the Presidency. It was to this quiet hideaway that he had come in the spring of 1945. It was here that he chose to pose for his official portrait.

As Elizabeth Shoumatoff was working on that painting on April 15, the President suffered a massive cerebral hemorrhage. He was taken to his bedroom and there he died a few moments later.

It was from this town that Franklin Roosevelt made his final journey, a trip that has been documented in photographs and news reports. And it is this town that still clings to the time when a President called it his home.

The Little White House is open from 9 a.m.-5 p.m. daily. It is closed on Thanksgiving and Christmas. Guides at The Little White House suggest that you arrive no later than 4 p.m. to give yourself plenty of time to see everything.

Admission charges to The Little White House are $4 for adults and $2 for children.

The Little White House isn't the only thing to see in Warm Springs, Ga. The town itself experienced a revival a few years ago, bringing a number of shops and craft stores to fill the streets that Roosevelt knew so well.

More to See and Do

Franklin D. Roosevelt State Park, Pine Mountain. One of the largest parks in the system, this facility offers a look at many historic buildings in addition to the "usual" park activities—swimming, hiking, picnicking and camping.

How to Get There

Warm Springs is in west central Georgia, about 30 miles northeast of Columbus on U.S. 27.

Where to Stay

Davis Inn, Pine Mountain. Accommodations range from inn-type rooms to efficiencies and suites.

Hotel Warm Springs, Warm Springs. Bette Davis slept here. And so did all the other dignitaries and guests of Roosevelt when he was at The Little White House. The Secret Service men also stayed at this hotel, built in 1907. Today it is a Bed and Breakfast and the owners say they've tried to leave everything as it was in Roosevelt's day "as much as possible." For the convenience of the hotel's more up-to-date guests, each room has its own private bath (Some of them do still have the bathtubs that were there in 1907.) and its own heating and cooling system.

Where to Eat

Victorian Tea Room, Warm Springs. Housed in one of Warm Springs' restored buildings, the Tea Room is open daily for lunch.

For More Information

For information about The Little White House, call 1-706-655-5870. For more information about Warm Springs, call 1-706-655-2558.

Roosevelt's Little White House in Warm Springs

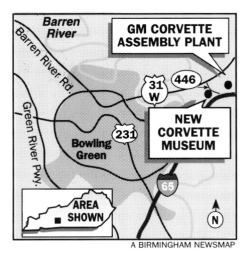

A BIRMINGHAM NEWSMAP

BOWLING GREEN, KENTUCKY

●●●

The National Corvette Museum

It's one of those rare places where you can see dreams taking shape. At one time or another, almost every red-blooded American has envisioned himself at the wheel of a Corvette. In Bowling Green, Kentucky, workers see to it that those Corvettes are there for the driving.

Perched on the edge of I-65, the plant is the only one that builds Corvettes. The assembly line there produces about 12 shiny new autos an hour, ushering about 96 Corvettes into the world each day.

Twice a day (at 9 a.m. and 1 p.m.), the public can enter that world where the daydream becomes steel. The one-hour tour takes visitors through the making of the car from frame to finish.

Three kinds of Corvettes—the coupe, the convertible and the ZR-1—are made at the plant. The car comes in 10 colors—with red being the most popular, followed by black and white.

More than 2,500 parts go into the 3,200-pound auto. The parts come from as far away as Australia (where the brakes are made) and as close as two miles (where the manufacturers find the convertible tops).

Making the powerful car requires a lot of room and a lot of effort. Under the roof of the plant there's enough room for 22 football fields. The building is cooled by a heat pump that produces

9,000 tons of cooling.

Some hints for visiting the plant: Call ahead for reservations if you have a group of 10 or more, wear comfortable shoes and remember, cameras aren't allowed. The plant is closed for holidays and during model changes.

Nearby is the National Corvette Museum, which had its official opening day during Labor Day weekend, 1994. The 68,000-square foot museum salutes 41 years of Corvettes and Corvette lovers. Among the museum exhibits are the one millionth Corvette produced at Bowling Green on July 2, 1992, concept Corvettes, racing Corvettes and celebrities from Corvette's "family tree." The museum is open from 9 a.m. to 7 p.m. seven days a week. Admission is $8 for adults, $6 for senior citizens (55 years and older) and $4 for children 6 to 16 years old.

More to See and Do

Riverview. The Civil War-era mansion has been restored and furnished to show the everyday life of a prosperous southern Kentucky family in the mid and late 1800s. Hours are 10 a.m. to 4 p.m. Tuesday through Saturday and 1 to 4 p.m. Sunday. Riverview is closed on Mondays, holidays and during the month of January. Admission is $3.50.

The Kentucky Museum. The museum houses everything from Victorian nursery toys to a spoon that is said to have been used by Pretty Boy Floyd during a jail break. Hours are 9:30 a.m. to 4 p.m. Tuesday through Saturday and 1 to 4 p.m. Sunday. The museum is closed Monday and, since it is on the campus of Western Kentucky University, is closed most university holidays. Admission is $2.

How to Get There

Bowling Green is in southwest Kentucky off I-65 on U.S. 231.

Where to Stay

Howard Johnson. Indoor pool, lawn games. Non-smoking rooms available. Located near Corvette plant.

Best Western Motor Inn. Indoor and outdoor pool, lawn games. Non-smoking rooms available.

Shaker Tavern, South Union. About 10 miles west of Bowling Green, the 1869 Shaker Tavern is a bed and breakfast. It is open March 15 through November 15.

Camping is available at Beech Bend and KOA.

Where to Eat
440 Main Restaurant and Bar. Set in restored historic building. Serves lunch and dinner Monday through Friday, dinner on Saturday.

Mariah's. Located in one of Bowling Green's oldest brick homes. Serves lunch and dinner daily.

For More Information
For more information about the Corvette Museum, call 1-502-781-7973. For more information about Bowling Green, call 1-502-782-0800.

Mint condition Corvette in street-scene setting at the Corvette Museum

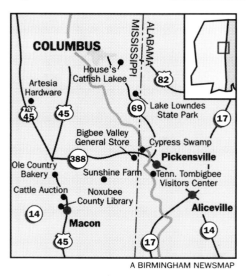

A BIRMINGHAM NEWSMAP

COLUMBUS, MISSISSIPPI

❂ ❂ ❂

Friendship Cemetery

Imagine being able to walk through a cemetery and hear the stories of the people buried there—sometimes from the people themselves. Something like that happens every year at Friendship Cemetery in Columbus, Miss.

At the "weeping angel" monument a mother tells the tale of her wonderful son, a community minister. He was so well loved for his good works, that at his death, she will tell you, the angels wept.

At another grave, a former slave tells a story of hardship. At another, one of the city's early businessmen tells how he gained his fortune.

At their graves, the city planners tell how Columbus came to be and educators buried in Friendship tell the stories of the birth of the Mississippi University for Women.

These insights into lives that ended long ago don't come through seances or mystical powers, they come through lots of research and hard work on the part of students at Mississippi School for Mathematics and Science.

Each student researches the life of a person buried in Friendship and, during Spring Pilgrimage, becomes that person during candlelight tours of the cemetery. Dressed in appropriate costumes and standing next to "their" tombstones, the students give visitors a unique look at Columbus history.

Friendship Cemetery itself is steeped in history—and worth a daylight visit any time of the year. It was here in April, 1866, that local women held a Decoration Day to honor the Civil War dead—Confederate and Union—by placing flowers on the soldiers' graves. That first observance, honoring troops on both sides of the battle, grew to become the nation's Memorial Day, when the dead from all wars are remembered.

The story of Columbus' Decoration Day says that the women arrived at the cemetery, carrying flowers cut from their gardens. As they placed the bouquets on the Confederate graves, they watched one young widow, Elizabeth Augusta Sykes, walk to the Union section of the cemetery and begin placing flowers on the graves there. The others followed her lead.

The graves of the Union soldiers now have been moved to national cemeteries, but Mrs. Sykes' charitable act is remembered each year on April 25th—Decoration Day at Friendship Cemetery.

More to See and Do
Blewett-Harrison-Lee Museum. The museum has exhibits on local history as well as many with emphasis on the Civil War. Open Tuesday and Thursday afternoons. No admission charge.

How to Get There
Columbus is in northeast Mississippi about six miles from the Alabama/Mississippi border on U.S. 82

Where to Stay
Comfort Inn. Complimentary Continental breakfast. Non-smoking rooms available.

Holiday Inn. Non-smoking rooms available.

Hampton Inn. Non-smoking rooms available.

Camping is available at Lake Lowndes State Park.

Where to Eat
Harvey's. Set in restored tannery. Children's meals available. Serves lunch and dinner.

Kountry Kitchen. Home-cooked meals. Serves breakfast and lunch.

Old Hickory Steakhouse. Children's meals available. Serves dinner only.

For More Information

For more information about Columbus, call the Convention and Visitors Bureau, 1-800-327-2686.

Friendship Cemetery has many stories to tell

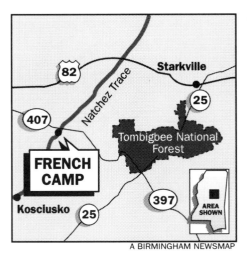

A BIRMINGHAM NEWSMAP

FRENCH CAMP, MISSISSIPPI

◉ ◉ ◉

When the Natchez Trace, now a National Parkway, wasn't much more than a buffalo trail, citizens were encouraged to establish "stands" along the route from what now is Jackson to northeastern Mississippi.

Louis LeFleur, living in the Jackson area, moved his family to what must have been "the wilds," about 90 miles north of Jackson to build an inn in 1812. Because LeFleur was French-Canadian, the stand he founded quickly became known as Frenchman's Camp and later as French Camp.

In 1821, Presbyterian missionaries from New England and began teaching the young people in the area, putting French Camp ahead of its time in education. In 1885, Scotch-Irish Christians from South Carolina established a boarding school there. The school has changed hands a few times, but it's been there ever since.

Today, French Camp is an interesting mix of old and new and remains a place that welcomes travelers along the Trace. French Camp Academy has become a place of refuge and learning for young people with family problems. Community children attend the school as well.

And, according to the school's president, the welcome mat is out for visitors. A not-to-be missed spot on the campus is Rainwater Observatory.

The observatory, with what is said to be the largest telescope between Atlanta and Houston, sits on an isolated hilltop in Choctaw County. It offers visitors the telescope and more than a dozen other instruments for daytime and nighttime viewing. The observatory is open by appointment for individuals and groups.

French Camp, according to French Camp Bed and Breakfast innkeeper Sallie Williford, "is a town of about 300 people. This part of the state is beautiful, there are hills and these two-lane roads are so pretty." Mrs. Williford, who grew up in Bessemer, said the move she and her husband made from Jackson a few years ago put her back in a "hilly place, not mountainous like Birmingham, but at least, hills." She admitted that it was hard to adjust to living on the "level ground" she found in Jackson.

French Camp has that small town feel, so much in fact that a boardwalk connects just about everything that would come under the heading of "attraction" there.

Just off the Trace is Huffman Log Cabin, an 1840 dogtrot cabin that today serves as a Visitor's Center. A porch behind the cabin leads to a boardwalk that takes visitors past the place where an ornate carriage belonging to Greenwood LeFlore (Louis LeFleur's son and a Mississippi State Senator) is displayed.

LeFlore used the carriage to travel twice to Washington, D.C.

The boardwalk next goes to the Drane House. Col. James Drane, son of a Revolutionary War soldier, was a political leader and early settler. He built the plantation-style home in 1846 using a water-powered saw.

French Camp Bed and Breakfast Inn is at the end of the boardwalk.

The B&B Mrs. Williford and her husband, both staff members at the Academy, own is pretty much the only game in town when it comes to accommodations. The inn is constructed of two 100-year-old log cabins.

Camping is available at nearby Jeff Busby State park.

There are some interesting dining spots in French Camp. Of course, if you're a guest at the bed and breakfast, you can expect a full Southern breakfast each morning. For lunch, you might try the Council House Cafe, set in the last Choctaw Council House on the Trace.

The Academy Dining Hall welcomes guests as well. Open year-round, except for breaks between school sessions, the dining hall serves lunch from 11:30 a.m. to 12:30 p.m. and dinner from 5:30 to 6 p.m. The cost is $2 per person per meal.

How to Get There

French Camp is in northeastern Mississippi on the Natchez Trace Parkway about 20 miles northeast of Kosciusko.

For More Information

For more information about French Camp Academy, call 1-601-547-6482.

Huffman Cabin at the entrance to French Camp visitors center

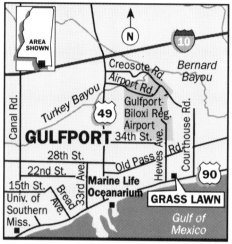

A BIRMINGHAM NEWSMAP

GULFPORT, MISSISSIPPI

❂❂❂

Grass Lawn

The visitors arrived just as the historic home was about to close for public tours. Outside, the sun was getting ready to set and shadows filled the front hall of Grass Lawn in Gulfport, Mississippi.

Grass Lawn, a Southern summer home, was built in 1836. The home features 10-foot wide galleries supported by two-story box columns and is a regular stop for those touring Gulfport.

"Just let us rush through and look quickly, please" they begged the tour guide. "We really want to see the house."

She consented and began a shorted version of her usual tour. While touring the first floor, one visitor asked, "Do you have any ghosts here?"

"Well, I won't say there are ghosts," was the answer. "All I can tell you is I close all the doors every night when I leave and every morning when I come back, they all are open."

After the visitors had seen the bottom floor, the guide invited them to quickly tour the upstairs unaccompanied. As they neared the top of the stairs, a bedroom door swung open by itself. Inside the room, a wardrobe door opened as the guests walked by.

The visitors left quickly, vowing never to ask permission to tour homes after hours again. "Maybe there was something there and maybe not," they said when they retold the story. "But if there was, it didn't want us there on its time."

For travelers who might like to check out the doors—and the rest of the house—at Grass Lawn, the house is open Monday, Wednesday and Friday from 10 a.m. to 4 p.m.

More to See and Do

Marine Life Oceanarium and Harbor Tour. The Oceanarium is home to sea lions, dolphins and other sea creatures. A fall or winter visit is especially enjoyable since the crowds are lighter and the animals, missing their usual audiences, are eager to perform. Marine Life is open from 9 a.m. to 4 p.m. seven days a week. A ticket also includes a tour of Gulfport Small Craft Harbor.

The Sullivan-Ryan Fight Site. In one of the last "bare-knuckles" fights, John Sullivan defeated Paddy Ryan in an 11-minute fight on February 7, 1882. Sullivan became heavyweight champion of the world with his victory. The spot where the fight was held eventually became a parking lot. There's a historic marker at U.S. 90 and Texas Avenue.

How to Get There

Gulfport is on the Mississippi Gulf Coast, on U.S. 90, about 13 miles west of Biloxi.

Where to Stay

Best Western Beach View Inn. Overlooks the harbor. Non-smoking rooms available.

Holiday Inn - Beachfront. Opposite the beach. Non-smoking rooms available.

Father Ryan's Bed and Breakfast, Biloxi.

Camping is available at Gulf Islands National Seashore.

Where to Eat

Montana's Bar-B-Que and Seafood. Eating at Montana's is a total experience. First there is the food, served buffet style and in huge quantities. Diners usually find they want to try more than they can consume in one visit to the restaurant. The desserts are generously sized and just as tasty as the other courses. Add to all of that the antiques (many of them for sale) that line the walls and an outing to Montana's becomes a time for eating, learning and even shopping. It's open 11 a.m. to 9 p.m. Tuesday through Sunday.

Vrazel's. It's hard to say what's best about Vrazel's—the food or the service. Both are extraordinary in this "fine dining" establishment. Many local residents go there regularly just to have the Eggplant La Rosa, a vegetable and seafood dish.

For More Information

For more information about Gulfport, call 1-800-237-9493.

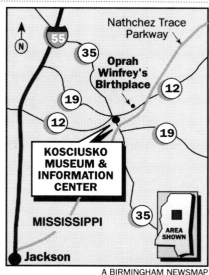

A BIRMINGHAM NEWSMAP

KOSCIUSKO, MISSISSIPPI

◉ ◉ ◉

In a region where city names seem so Southern—Farm Haven, Laurel Hill, Walnut Grove, Poplar Creek—how does a town named Kosciusko come to be? In truth, the spot along the Natchez Trace once had one of those more southern names—Red Bud Springs. Since the mid-1800's, however, it has honored a Polish patriot.

Tadeusz Kosciuszko was born in Lithuania in 1746 and attended the Warsaw Cadet School. He was commissioned a captain in Poland after he completed his military studies in schools in Germany, Italy and France.

When, in 1776, Kosciuszko heard about the American Revolution, he came to American to offer his services. He was commissioned by the Continental Congress and became a brigadier general in 1783. During the last part of the Revolution, the Polish general served in the South.

After the war, Kosciuszko returned to Poland where he led his country to the adoption of a new constitution. During the resulting uprising with Prussia and Russia, he was wounded and captured, spending two years in a prison camp. He was released on the condition that he never return to Poland.

Kosciuszko came to the United States where he died in 1817, still longing for his native country.

When William Dodd, the first representative of Attala County to the Mississippi Legislature, was given the honor of renaming the town that once was Red Bud Springs, his thoughts turned to his grandfather's Revolutionary War stories.

Dodd's grandfather had served with Kosciuszko under Nathaniel Green and it seemed natural to Dodd to suggest that the Mississippi town bear the name of the man Thomas Jefferson called "as pure a son of liberty as I have ever known." (But in naming the town, it somehow got spelled "Kosciusko.")

The story of Tadeusz Kosciuszko and his place in American history is told at the Kosciuszko Museum and Information Center near the Natchez Trace Parkway. Exhibits at the museum include permanent displays as well as changing presentations that tell the story of Kosciuszko the man and Kosciusko the city.

More to See and Do

Buffalo United Methodist Community Center. The building that now houses the Buffalo United Methodist Church's Community Center originally was the church building. It's the church Oprah Winfrey attended during her Kosciusko childhood.

Kosciusko City Cemetery. There are many late 19th century markers here, including the one for Laura Kelly. The marker, a statue of Mrs. Kelly, was erected by her husband so he could view it from the window of his home.

How to Get There

Kosciusko is in central Mississippi, about 60 miles northeast of Jackson just off the Natchez Trace Parkway on Mississippi 12.

Where to Stay

Best Western Parkway Inn. Non-smoking rooms available.

Days Inn. Non-smoking rooms available.

Redbud Inn. A bed and breakfast set in a historic home.

Lucas Hill. A bed and breakfast set in a historic Greek Revival home.

Camping is available at Holmes County State Park.

Where to Eat

Cafe on the Square. Features homemade soups, breads and desserts. Serves breakfast and lunch Monday through Saturday.

Redbud Tea Room. Serves lunch Monday through Friday.

For More Information

For more information about Kosciusko, call 1-601-289-2981.

A BIRMINGHAM NEWSMAP

LELAND, MISSISSIPPI

●●●

"The Birthplace of the Frog"

Question—where is Kermit the Frog's birthplace?

Answer—if famous frogs do indeed have hometowns, then surely Kermit's must be Greenville and Leland, Mississippi.

In 1934, Kermit's "grandfather," Paul Henson brought his family to Mississippi. He came to Stoneville (near Greenville and Leland) to work in the agricultural research labs at a federal facility there. Two years later, James Maury Henson was born in King's Daughters Hospital in Greenville.

For a few years, the family lived in cottages on the grounds of the Stoneville station. Then the Hensons were sent to another USDA research station in Maryland. They returned to Stoneville in 1943 and young Jim entered the second grade at Leland Elementary School.

Perhaps Kermit really had his beginnings as Jim played (and maybe watched frogs) along the banks of Deer Creek after classes. Wherever Henson first started thinking about frogs and puppets, he once gave the city an autographed picture of himself—surrounded by muppets and signed "To Leland—Birthplace of the Frog."

Henson and his family left Mississippi in the summer of 1948, but the city of Leland never has completely let go of this native son.

Leland now is the home of the Jim Henson Exhibit, something the townfolk hope will grow into the "The Birthplace of The Frog." At the exhibit are some of Kermit's best friends as well as Henson family pictures and Muppet memorabilia.

A video center at the exhibit shows Muppet movies and some of Jim Henson's early works, including "Sam and Friends." That local five-minute show, aired in Washington, D.C., was the one that introduced Jim Henson's Muppets to the world.

The exhibit is open Monday through Friday from 10 a.m. to 4 p.m. From Memorial Day to Labor Day, the exhibit also is open from 1 to 5 p.m. on Saturday and Sunday.

More to See and Do

Deer Creek. Deer Creek is famous for its role in Civil War battles when Union forces tried to navigate this narrow waterway in an attempt to outflank Vicksburg. Today visitors see Leland's historic district in the old homes along the banks of Deer Creek. The creek also runs through the town and is home to ducks and geese.

How to Get There

Leland is in northwestern Mississippi about eight miles east of Greenville on U.S. 82.

Where to Stay

Ramada Inn, Greenville. Non-smoking rooms available.

Hampton Inn, Greenville. Non-smoking rooms available.

Camping is available at Warfield Point Park, Greenville.

Where to Eat

Lillo's, Leland. Owned by the Lillo family and noted for its Italian food.

Cicero's, Leland. Locally owned, features barbecue, steaks and seafood.

Shelton House Restaurant, Greenville.

For More Information

For more information about Leland, call 1-601-686-2687. For more information about Greenville, call 1-601-378-3141.

Kermit, a good ole Mississippi frog, made good and put Leland on the map

A BIRMINGHAM NEWSMAP

OCEAN SPRINGS, MISSISSIPPI

❂❂❂

In the world of the Mississippi Coast, bright and glittery with its casinos, the town of Ocean Springs seems to march to the beat of a different drummer. The glitz, the hustle and bustle are absent. The appeal to visitors isn't.

Ocean Springs, though a more slow-paced, relaxing spot than the dazzling casinos just minutes away, still is a town where things do happen and there's plenty to see and do.

People in this town find time to visit at the local cafe, where a group of morning diners meet each day to solve the problems of the world. They have time to drop in at Favorites, the book store, to find out what's happening in the literary world of Ocean Springs.

They have time to stroll from place to place along the streets lined with shops and boutiques and either window-shop or do some actual purchasing.

Visitors who want to slip into character and become a part of the town for a while need to begin with a stop at the Chamber of Commerce office, located in the Old Louisville and Nashville Railroad Depot. When the depot was built in 1907, it quickly became the hub of the town's activities. It's quickly becoming the city's center once again.

Listed on the National Register of Historic Places, the depot is home not only to the Chamber of Commerce but a couple of spe-

119

cialty shops where the merchandise has a definite local flavor.

The Gayle Clark Gallery, run by Ms. Clark, a noted Mississippi metalsmith and jeweler, sells not only her work, but that of other American craftsmen.

Realizations, with its Walter Anderson Shop, offers clothing, fabrics and prints of the Southern artist's block print designs.

Books, reproductions and posters also are available at the store.

Armed with the Chamber's brochures on walking and driving tours, bicycle trails, "tree" tours, shopping and dining, it only takes a few minutes to come under the spell of the town. Visitors quickly find themselves eager to discover what's around the next corner and reluctant to leave the secluded quiet of Ocean Springs.

More to See and Do

Walter Anderson Museum of Art. The collection includes mural, paintings, ceramics and sculptures by Anderson, the eccentric artist who made Ocean Springs his home. Open 10 a.m. to 5 p.m. Tuesday through Saturday; 1 to 5 p.m. Sunday. Admission is $3 for adults; $1 for children 6-12.

The Doll House. The blue and white Victorian home was built not for humans to live in, but for dolls to inhabit. The six viewing rooms are filled with antique dolls, modern dolls, marionettes, character dolls and stuffed animals. Open 1 to 5 p.m. Tuesday through Sunday. Admission is by donation to benefit the YMCA Pet Shelter Fund.

How to get there

Ocean Springs is on the Mississippi coast about five miles east of Biloxi on U.S. 90.

Where to Stay

Oak Shade Bed and Breakfast. The bed and breakfast room, adjacent to the house (originally the home of the Ocean Springs Harbor Master) has a sitting area, kitchen nook and bedroom area. There is a television, refrigerator and microwave and coffee maker. Breakfast is a "continental plus," with fruit, pastries and cereal in the room for the guests to choose from.

Seven Oaks Gulf Hills Country Club. This resort offers a secluded retreat for the traveler. Non-smoking rooms available.

Camping is available at Gulf Islands National Seashore.

Where to Eat

Anthony's Under the Oaks. The restaurant, in a lovely house overlooking the bayou, not only offers fine dining, but a view of the local seagulls and pelicans. Serves lunch and dinner.

Martha's Tea Room. Enjoy lunch in a Victorian home, the setting for the restaurant. Homemade breads and desserts are served up daily and there are daily specials.

For More Information

For more information about Ocean Springs, call 1-601-875-4424.

Ocean Springs, Miss., pelicans perch atop pilings

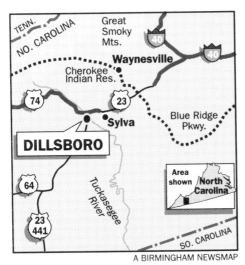

A BIRMINGHAM NEWSMAP

DILLSBORO, NORTH CAROLINA

⊚ ⊚ ⊚

With the pace of today's hectic lifestyles where fax machines, cellular phones, computers and pages connect us constantly with our responsibilities, it's no wonder that, from time to time, everyone looks for a getaway.

If you're one of those searching for little peace and quiet, you might consider a visit to Dillsboro, North Carolina, where, as one recent visitor put it, "we were forced to relax."

There aren't a lot of malls, theaters and other glitzy attractions there, she pointed out, but it was "exactly the trip we were looking for."

Dillsboro, which sits among hills and waterfalls in North Carolina's Jackson County, was founded when William Allen and Alice Enloe Dills moved from nearby Webster and built a house there in 1882. By 1888, Dillsboro was a stop on the Western North Carolina Railroad and had become the county's center of commercial activity.

It had six general stores, two sawmills, two clay mines and a variety of other businesses.

The booming growth of the city was cut short by one of the things that made it so appealing—a river that flowed near the town.

By the turn of the century, three floods had wiped out a number of thriving businesses in Dillsboro and much of its industry relocated in nearby Sylva.

A lot of the good things about that era in Dillsboro history still are around to be enjoyed today. The city retains many of its original buildings and much of its original flavor.

Even though the town moves at a slightly slower pace than that of larger cities, the traveler said, there still are signs that old meets new there from time to time.

"They showed us where one of the scenes from the movie 'The Fugitive' was filmed," the visitor said. "It's not far from Dillsboro."

More to See and Do

Riverwood Shops. This collection of six shops in Dillsboro showcases the work of local artists. Among the items found there are handcrafted pewter goods, rosewood fountain pens, blown glass, pottery and wall hangings. There also is a rare edition and second-hand bookstore.

How to Get There

Dillsboro is southwest of Asheville on U.S. 23/441. Check before you travel as some roads close in the winter due to snow.

Where to Stay

The Dillsboro Inn. A three-story A-frame, the inn is situated on the Tuckasegee River overlooking a waterfall. The inn, open year-round, has four guest rooms in the main house and two efficiency units. A full country breakfast is included.

Squire Watkins Inn. Built in 1885, this Queen Anne-style house was home to J.C. Watkins, a local magistrate. The inn has five guest rooms and rates include a full breakfast. Cottages also are available.

Mountain Brook Cottages. This facility offers guests 12 cottages, a spa and sauna bungalow, nature trail, game room and picnic and bonfire area.

Camping is available at Fort Tatham Campsites in Sylva (Campground is open April through October).

Where to Eat

Bradley's General Store. Dillsboro's historic country store features an old-fashioned soda fountain where lunch is served April through December.

Dillsboro Smokehouse. Located in the heart of the shopping district, the restaurant specializes in hickory smoked barbecue.

The Jarrett House. Family-style Southern meals are a tradition here. The restaurant is open from mid-April to October.

The Well House. The restaurant specializes in hot deli sandwiches.

For More Information

For more information about Dillsboro, call 1-800-962-1911.

A BIRMINGHAM NEWSMAP

BELVIDERE, TENNESSEE

◉◉◉

Falls Mill

Where would you go to find an industrial engineering professor and a woman with a degree in sociology and anthropology? How about a college campus? Better yet, how about a water-powered mill tucked away in the woods in Tennessee?

John and Janie Lovett decided years ago that they wanted to buy an old mill and when they saw Falls Mill near Belvidere, "we knew that was it," according to Janie.

John, who has given up the academic life to spend his days as a mill keeper, spends a great deal of time repairing and restoring the mill equipment. Lugging around stone and metal is a far cry from the college classroom, but it's one that must agree with Lovett and his wife.

John seems content to work with the machines that make his mill produce stone-ground flour and meal on a regular basis. The Lovetts buy grains from local farmers and use the century-old waterwheel to turn the antique equipment that grinds corn meal, grits and wheat, rye and rice flours.

Also housed at the mill is the Museum of Power and Industry, a growing exhibit of machinery from the 1800s.

Janie has done the research that brings the mill's history to life. Falls Mill, built in 1873, has been a cotton spinning and wool carding factory, a cotton gin, a wood-working shop and a grist mill.

And, while it still is a grist mill, it now has become a part of a

125

complex the Lovetts hope to develop over the years. They've already added three more buildings—an 1895 log cabin, a log carriage house and an 1836 stagecoach inn, all in various stages of reconstruction.

"We have lots of plans, like expanding our grain sales, restoring the stage coach inn, developing a nature trail, building a blacksmith shop," Janie said. "We love it here—there's nowhere else we'd rather be."

The mill and its museum are open for tours Monday through Saturday from 9 a.m. to 4 p.m. and Sunday from 12:30 to 4 p.m. Admission is $2 for adults, $1.50 for senior citizens and $1 for children under 14.

More to See and Do

Winchester's Rainbow Row, Winchester. This collection of stores is housed in a recently restored 19th century building. Here shoppers can find antiques, books, gifts and gourmet foods and coffees.

How to Get There

Falls Mill is not far from Huntsville, Alabama. To reach Fall's Mill from Huntsville, take I-565 North to U.S. 72. Take U.S. 72 East to Moore's Mill Road. Turn left onto Moore's Mill Road and take that road to Winchester Road. Turn right onto Winchester Road and go about 30 miles to the town of Huntland. Turn left in Huntland and continue to follow the signs toward Winchester. Turn left off U.S. 64 at Old Salem and follow the signs to the mill.

Where to Stay

Falls Mill Log Cabin. A bed and breakfast located in the Lovetts' restored log cabin. Adjacent to the mill.

The Antebellum Inn, Winchester. A bed and breakfast.

Camping is available at Tims Ford State Park, near Winchester.

Where to Eat

The Antebellum Inn. Serves lunch Monday, Wednesday and Friday; brunch on Sunday and dinner Thursday through Saturday.

The Belvidere Market. The specialty is the "Belvidere Bomber" sandwich, highly recommended by local folks. Open for lunch.

The Swiss Pantry, Belvidere. Cakes, breads and cheeses are the specialty here, but you'll find lots more to enjoy as well. Open Tuesday through Friday from 7 a.m. to 5 p.m. and Saturday from 8 a.m. to 4 p.m.

For More Information

For more information about Falls Mill, call 1-615-469-7161. For more information about Winchester, call 1-615-967-6788.

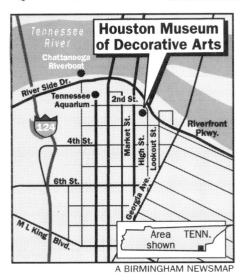

Houston Museum of Decorative Arts

Tennessee River

Chattanooga Riverboat

River Side Dr.

Tennessee Aquarium

2nd St.

124

4th St.

Market St.

High St.

Lookout St.

Riverfront Pkwy.

6th St.

Georgia Ave.

M L King Blvd.

Area TENN. shown

A BIRMINGHAM NEWSMAP

CHATTANOOGA, TENNESSEE

◉◉◉

Houston Museum

Sometimes people who seem to be single minded in their devotion to something are considered to be very smart, other times, they might be branded as extremely eccentric. Anna Safley Houston, it turns out, was both.

From a fascination with glass as a child grew Mrs. Houston's collection of glassware, antiques, music boxes and textiles that number in the tens of thousands. When Mrs. Houston died, she willed her collection to the city of Chattanooga and the University of Chattanooga. It took a while for anyone to recognize the worth of the items, but today they enjoy a home at the Houston Museum of Decorative Arts in Chattanooga.

Mrs. Houston was married numerous times—some reports put it at as few as five, others as many as 10—but her real love always was her collection, perhaps because she seems to have made better choices for her collection than for her marriage partners.

A fiercely independent woman, Mrs. Houston successfully operated an antique business that she opened in 1920. While she ran the store, she was gathering the pieces that would become her collection. She didn't have the benefit of a formal education, but she educated herself on the subject of glassware through reading, watching and listening. When Mrs. Houston added a piece to her collection, it wasn't just because she liked the piece. It was because she liked the piece—and the piece was valuable.

When the Depression came she was forced to close her store. While she was willing to give up the store in her home, she wouldn't part with one piece of her collection. Even when it came to a choice between selling part of the collection and selling her house, she chose to do without the house.

She enlisted the help of a young boy in the neighborhood to build a barn where she and her collection would live. Mrs. Houston slept on the floor of the barn, unwilling to take up any floor space with a bed—that space, she reasoned would be better used as housing for pieces of her collection.

When space in the barn got tight, she hung her 15,000-piece pitcher collection from the roof of the barn.

After Mrs. Houston's death, the collection sat unwanted and unappreciated in the barn. The weight of the pitchers at one point pulled the roof down and broke many of the pieces. For ten years, the Staffordshire, Dresden, Tiffany, Baccarat, Wedgwood and Mettlach sat alongside Regina music boxes in the barn.

Finally, a not-for-profit organization was formed to receive Mrs. Houston's collection and house it in a museum. The Houston Museum of Decorative Art is open from 10 a.m. to 4:30 p.m. Tuesday through Saturday and from 2 to 4:30 p.m. Sunday. There is no admission charge, but a donation is requested.

How to Get There

Chattanooga is in south central Tennessee on I-24.

To reach the Houston Museum, take Market Street to Fourth Street (near the Tennessee Aquarium). Take Fourth Street East to High Street. Turn north on High. The museum is at 201 High Street.

Where to Stay

Days Inn Rivergate. Complimentary coffee in the lobby.

Comfort Hotel River Plaza.

Camping is available at Raccoon Mountain Campground.

Where to Eat

Town and Country Restaurant. A family dining tradition for more than 40 years. Serves lunch and dinner.

Sandbar Restaurant. Overlooks the river. Traditional American cuisine. Serves lunch and dinner.

LeDoux's Classic French Restaurant. Serves lunch Monday through Friday, dinner Thursday through Saturday, Sunday brunch. Reservations requested.

For More Information

For more information about Chattanooga, call the Convention and Visitors Bureau at 1-800-322-3344.

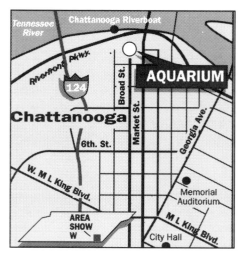

CHATTANOOGA, TENNESSEE

❦❦❦

Tennessee Aquarium

It may sound impossible, but you can see the Tennessee River—from the Appalachian high country where it begins, to the Mississippi Delta, all in one day. And you don't have to do view it from an airplane.

In fact, you get a much closer look than you'd have in a plane.

"The Tennessee Aquarium give visitors their first look at the underwater world of the river," explained an Aquarium official. "Most people have seen saltwater fish in their ocean habitats, but few have seen freshwater fish in their natural environment—the rushing water, the quiet pools and nooks and crannies along the river shoreline."

The Aquarium sits along the banks of the Tennessee River in downtown Chattanooga. The 130,000-square foot structure, which is as high as a 12-story building, holds 400,000 gallons of water. There are more than 3,500 living specimens of animals and plants on display there.

Animals seen at the Aquarium include many varieties of bass and trout, paddlefish and gar, river otters, kingfishers, songbirds, waterfowl, alligators and snapping turtles. Visitors also will see Piranha, tigerfish, pike, sharks, stingrays and tarpon.

The Aquarium is divided into five major galleries— Appalachian Cove Forest, Tennessee River Gallery, Discovery Falls, Mississippi Delta and Rivers of the World.

The Appalachian Cove Forest, which re-creates the Tennessee River's source, has fish, otters and free-flying birds. The Tennessee River Gallery looks at the river at midstream. In this area is one of the world's largest freshwater tanks, filled with more than 30 species of fish. A series of interactive displays and small tanks, Discovery Falls shows visitors the river's interdependent ecosystem. Alligators, coastal birds, amphibians and reptiles inhabit the Mississippi Delta area. Here, too, is the Aquarium's only saltwater exhibit, a large tank devoted to the Gulf of Mexico. Rivers of the World compares six other river systems to the Tennessee.

The Aquarium's galleries are connected by its 60-foot-high central canyon. After moving through each gallery, visitors enter the canyon, which contains a series of ramps and bridges linking all five levels of the building.

And visitors never are far from a view of the "real thing." The Tennessee River, flowing just outside the Aquarium, is visible from the lobby as well as from windows and patios located on several floors.

Aquarium hours are 10 a.m.-6 p.m. daily. There are extended hours on summer weekends. Admission is $9.75 for adults, $5.75 for children 3-12.

More to See and Do

TVA Energy Center. Hands-on exhibits and interactive computer games show how TVA produces energy and how people use it. Open 8 a.m. to 4:30 p.m., Monday through Saturday. Admission is free.

Lake Winnepsaukah Amusement Park. More than 30 rides, attractions and games fill this park, located about 10 miles from Chattanooga. The park is open Thursday through Sunday, May through August. In April and September, it is open weekends only.

How to Get There

Chattanooga is in south central Tennessee on I-24. To reach the Tennessee Aquarium, take the Broad Street exit off I-24. Go north on Broad Street to the Aquarium.

Where to Stay

Chattanooga Marriott.

Days Inn Lookout Mountain.

Adams Hilborne. Guest rooms set in an historic home.

Camping is available at Chester Frost Park.

Where to Eat

Mom's Italian Villa. Serves lunch and dinner. Reservations recommended.

Porker's BBQ. Serves lunch and dinner.

Vine Street Market. Known for its desserts. Serves lunch and dinner.

For More Information

For more information about Chattanooga, call the Convention and Visitors Bureau at 1-800-322-3344. For more information about the Tennessee Aquarium, call 1-423-266-3467.

Aquarium has been a major part of revitalizing Chattanooga tourism

133

A BIRMINGHAM NEWSMAP

CHATTANOOGA, TENNESSEE

◉◉◉

Tennessee Valley Railroad

Ah, the romance of the train. The gentle swaying of the cars as they rock through the country-side. The sound of the wheels as they meet the metal rails.

Railroading in America had its "golden age," a half-century filled with railroad empires, luxurious travel and trains that each sought to outdo the other in comfort and service. It was a time when every-one who was anyone took the train.

Those years —from 1900 to 1950—are recaptured today at the Tennessee Valley Rail-road Museum, which sits not all that far from downtown Chattanooga. And the nice thing about this museum is that it not only includes such things as an audio-visual exhibit about trains, it includes operating trains as well.

The railroad, billed as the largest operating historic railroad in the South, was founded in 1961 to preserve operating steam pas-senger trains. Today, it includes not only track that is used regular-ly and trains that run along it, but a collection of train cars, a repair shop, a dining room and a gift shop. And, as TVRR members like to say, "it's all presented in a setting that reflects an America of 60 years ago, except that we have clean restrooms and air conditioning."

The Tennessee Valley Railroad operates almost year-round, tak-ing riders along a route that follows much of the original right-of-way of the East Tennessee & Georgia Railroad. The East Tennessee

& Georgia served as a vital supply link first to the Confederacy, then to the Union as the tide of battle shifted in Chattanooga in November, 1863.

The Tennessee Valley Railroad has two stations in the Chattanooga area—Grand Junction and East Chattanooga. Daily service from 10 a.m. to 2 p.m. runs in April, May, September and October. (The East Chattanooga station is not open for this service.) Daily service from 10 a.m. to 5 p.m. runs in June through August. (Both stations are open from 30 minutes before the first train through 5 p.m.) Weekend service from 10 a.m. to 5 p.m. Saturday and from noon to 5 p.m. Sunday runs April through November. There also is a "Downtown Arrow" service between the Chattanooga Choo-Choo and the Grand Junction Station on the weekends from June through August.

From time to time, special excursions on the Tennessee Valley Railroad are planned. These take riders through areas such as northwest Georgia. The trains usually are made up of passenger cars, a commissary car and an on-board gift shop. Passengers also can choose, for an extra fee, to enjoy the trip from special accommodations.

Often the train will include the Clover Colony, a Pullman car used by Marilyn Monroe while filming scenes for "Some Like It Hot." And the office car Eden Isle is available for group charters of up to 12 people.

For more information or for reservations, call 1-423-894-8028.

How to Get There

Chattanooga is in south central Tennessee on I-24.

Both Tennessee Valley Railroad stations are near downtown Chattanooga. To reach the Grand Junction Station, take I-75 to Exit 4 (Highway 153). Drive north on Highway 153 to the Jersey Pike exit. Follow the signs from that exit to the station.

To reach the East Chattanooga Depot, go east on Main Street from downtown Chattanooga. Turn left on Holtzclaw Avenue and go north to Wilcox Boulevard (where the railroad crosses the intersection diagonally). Turn right on Wilcox, go to the third light and turn left on North Chamberlain. The depot is six blocks down on the right.

Where to Stay

Chattanooga Choo-Choo Holiday Inn. Set in Terminal Station. Some rooms in train cars. Non-smoking rooms available.

The Radisson Read House. A Chattanooga landmark. Non-smoking rooms available.

Bluff View Inn. A bed and breakfast.

Camping is available at Best Holiday Trav-L-Park and Shipp's Yogi Bear Jellystone Park Camp/Resort.

Where to Eat

The Loft. One of Chattanooga's fine dining establishments.

Big River Grille and Brewing Works. Set in a former trolley barn, the grill offers a menu of ribs, chicken and steak dishes. The beverage specialty is, of course, freshly brewed beers and ales.

Rib and Loin. One of the city's most popular barbecue restaurants.

For More Information

For more information about Chattanooga, call 1-800-322-3344.

A BIRMINGHAM NEWSMAP

COLUMBIA, TENNESSEE

❦❦❦

To the Greeks, the Athenaeum was a place of learning. In the Roman Empire, the Athenaeum was a school for studying the arts. The Athenaeum in Columbia, Tennessee, has been a residence and a school. Today it is a piece of history.

Begun in 1835 as a residence for Samuel Polk Walker, nephew of President James K. Polk, the Athenaeum was completed in 1837 as the home of Rev. Franklin Gillette Smith and his family. The Rev. Smith had come to Tennessee to be president of Columbia Female Institute, an Episcopal school for girls.

When, in 1851, the Rev. Smith resigned from the institute to begin Columbia Athenaeum School, the family home became the school's rectory. While the parlors became reception areas for the school, the bedrooms and an upstairs room were used by the Smith family.

The school stayed open until 1904 and today the Gothic/Moorish structure that served as the rectory is a reminder of the way things used to be. Much of the building, open for public tours Wednesday through Saturday, is furnished with pieces original to the home. Other pieces are from various members of the Smith family.

The Athenaeum is open from 11 a.m. to 5 p.m. Wednesday through Saturday and from 1 to 5 p.m. on Sunday.

More to See and Do

Rattle and Snap. Shortly after the American Revolution, Col. William Polk engaged the governor of North Carolina is a game of Rattle-and-Snap, a popular amusement of the time. Polk won the game and the tract of land where this house is built. The house is filled with period pieces, many from area Polk family homes. Rattle and Snap is open from 10 a.m. to 4 p.m. Tuesday through Saturday and from 1 to 4 p.m. Sunday. Admission is $7.50 for adults, $5 for senior citizens and $2.50 for children.

How to Get There

Columbia is in central Tennessee about 85 miles southwest of Nashville on U.S. 31.

Where to Stay

Days Inn. Complimentary Continental breakfast. Non-smoking rooms available.

Ramada Inn. Complimentary Continental breakfast. Non-smoking rooms available.

Oak Springs Inn and Gallery. A bed and breakfast.

Where to Eat

Backyard Barbecue. It's all drive-through service, but the local folks say the food is excellent.

Catfish Campus. Another local favorite.

Harlan House. Set in an old home in the heart of downtown Columbia.

For More Information

For more information about Columbia and Maury County, call 1-615-381-7176.

TENNESSEE — NORTH CAROLINA

Ice Mountain

68

Ducktown

64

Copperhill

McCaysville

60

5

76

Area shown

TENN.

GEORGIA

A BIRMINGHAM NEWSMAP

ICE MOUNTAIN, TENNESSEE

◉ ◉ ◉

Eagle Adventures

You say you've seen City Slickers II and, despite that, you still think you'd like to try a dude ranch vacation? Maybe the people at Eagle Adventure in Ice Mountain, Tennessee, will be a pleasant alternative to looking up those folks who booked Billy Crystal's outing.

The company offers a variety of ways to experience the great outdoors.

For guests who want that cowboy experience, there are campgrounds and a frontier-style bunkhouse on The Ranch. For those who think a little bit of roughing it is more than enough, there are private cabins (probably the best bet for families with children).

Some of the Eagle Adventure Outings are geared toward families with older children while others are designed for those with children five years old and older. On some of those outings, children will accompany parents and on others, the children are offered supervised activities while the parents take part in more adventuresome quests, such as white water rafting.

Among the adventurous outings offered by the company are:

Drawn Wagon and Horseback Campout. This two-day adventure is among those open to families with children five years old and older.

Nantahala River White Water Rafting. A guided outing, this rafting adventure includes some Class II rapids. This trip is open

139

to families with children five years old and older.

Great Smoky Mountain Railroad Excursion. This train trip takes travelers across Fontana Lake and through the Nantahala Gorge. This trip is open to families with children five years old and older.

Photo Adventure. This outing offers a tour aboard the raft bus following the Ocoee River Whitewater Trip. This trip is open to families with children five years old and older.

Tubing on the River. Take an easy float on the Toccoa River. This trip is open to families with children five years old and older.

Day on the Lake. Participants spend a day pontoon boating, swimming, fishing and picnicking. This trip is open to families with children five years old and older.

Horseback Riding Lesson and Pasture Ride. This outing is low-key and is open to families with children five years old and older.

Gold Prospecting. Participants search for their fortune at the site of the second gold discovery in North America. This trip is open to families with children five years old and older.

Cherokee Indian Reservation Visit. This outing includes tickets to the outdoor drama, "Unto These Hills," the story of the Trail of Tears. This trip is open to families with children five years old and older.

Raft the Wild Ocoee River. This guided outing involves a trip on the site of the 1996 Olympic White Water Events. The rapids here are Class III and IV. This trip is designed for families with children over 11 years old.

Rappelling. This trip is designed for families with children over 11 years old.

Championship Mountain Golf. This outing, on an 18-hole course, is designed for families with children over 11 years old.

Working Ranch Adventure. Participants can work alongside the river and wrangler staffs as they go about their rafting and trail-ride chores. They also get in on an authentic mountain horse and tack sale. This trip is designed for families with children over 11 years old.

Bass and Muskie Fishing on Lake Hiawassee. This trip is designed for families with children over 11 years old.

Check-in sites for the adventures vary. Guests who are staying in the bunkhouse or are camping out usually check in at the Ranch.

Those staying in a cabin check in at the company headquarters.

Prices for the adventures vary with the length of stay and with the accommodations. There's a Wrangler Price for those interested in camping and a City Slicker Price for those who want private, furnished lodging.

How to Get There

Ice Mountain and the Ranch are located in southeastern Tennessee near the intersection of Georgia 5 and Tennessee 68. The Eagle Adventures Offices (and check-in site for the cabins) is located at the Intersection of these two highways.

To continue to the ranch, take Tennessee 68 West to U.S. 64/74 (near Ducktown). Take U.S. 64/74 East three miles. There will be a sign at Mile Marker 29 indicating the turn onto the road leading to the ranch. Turn there and follow the signs to the ranch site.

For More Information

For more information about Eagle Adventure, call 1-800-288-EAGL.

A BIRMINGHAM NEWSMAP

LYNCHBURG, TENNESSEE

◉ ◉ ◉

When Jasper Newton (Jack) Daniel bought a small distillery in the hills of middle Tennessee in the 1860s, he vowed, "Every day we make it, we make it the best we can."

He must have done something right. Not only has his product sold pretty well, but more than 300,000 people come annually to have a look at how it's made.

A tour of the distillery begins in the Visitors' Center. Visitors simply come in, ask for a ticket (really a poker chip) for the next tour and wait for the trip through Jack Daniel's Land to begin. A word of caution—this trip isn't for those who can't climb stairs or manipulate hills. There are lots of ups and downs to the Tennessee whiskey business and most of them are laid out across hilly land.

Before the actual tour begins, visitors see a brief film in the Visitors Center and then leave to explore the distillery grounds with a guide who sounds like he learned the fine art of the English language straight from Helen Crump with a little bit of tutoring from Gomer and Goober.

Winding up, down and through the grounds, those taking the tour see where the charcoal for the filtering process is made, Cave Spring with its virtually lime-free water that's part of the Jack Daniel's recipe, where the whiskey is distilled, filtered and stored for aging and the original office where Jack Daniel held sway over his sour mash empire.

Just outside the office stands a life-size (5-foot-2) statue of Jack Daniel. The statue, you'll learn, is an exact replica of Daniel except for the feet, which had to be enlarged to give the statue a secure base.

The tour also now includes the newly opened brewery at Jack Daniel's. Visitors tour it after they've see the distillery.

The tour, which is free, takes about 90 minutes and a new tour begins every 15 minutes. The distillery is open daily except for Thanksgiving, Christmas Day and New Year's Day. Hours are 8 a.m. to 4 p.m.

More to See and Do

Moore County Courthouse. The courthouse, built in 1885, is constructed of bricks made in Lynchburg.

Moore County Jail. The jail is older than the courthouse. Local residents like to say that "any jailhouse with potted geraniums on the front porch is the sign of a well-run, law-abiding community."

Shopping. The town square is lined with places to shop in and explore. You'll find everything from hams to needlework, from Christmas ornaments to furniture.

How to Get There

Lynchburg is located on Tennessee 50 in south central Tennessee, about 50 miles northeast of Huntsville, AL.

Where to Stay

Best Western Old Fort Motor Inn, Manchester. Non-smoking rooms available.

Lynchburg Bed and Breakfast. A 19th century home within walking distance of the town square and the Jack Daniel's Distillery.

Tims Ford State Park, Winchester. Cabins and camping.

Where to Eat

The Countryside Restaurant. Serves lunch and dinner Monday through Friday and Sunday.

Miss Mary Bobo's Boarding House. Eat at mid-day in an 1850s colonial home where the meal is served family style. Daily menus include two meats, six fresh vegetables, homemade bread, dessert and beverage. Reservations are required. Make them early.

Iron Kettle Restaurant. Serves lunch Monday through Saturday.

The Pepper Patch. You won't get a full meal here, but you'll find all sorts of Tennessee-made food goods. One of the specialties is Tipsy Cake, which contains a sample of the city's most famous product.

For More Information

For more information about tours of the Jack Daniel's Distillery, call 1-615-759-4221. For more information about Lynchburg, write Lynchburg-Moore County Chamber of Commerce, Public Square, Courthouse, Lynchburg, TN 37352.

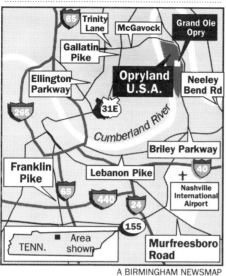

A BIRMINGHAM NEWSMAP

NASHVILLE, TENNESSEE

◉ ◉ ◉

It's the ultimate goal of those who want to make it big in the country music business. And it's the ultimate goal of those who want to make it big in Tennessee politics.

The city of Nashville is an interesting mix of country music twang and capital city sophistication. As such, it has a wealth of things to offer visitors and has become a destination for travelers from all over the world.

Of course, no visit to Nashville would complete without at least a peek into the country music business. Perhaps the best place to get an overview and thorough indoctrination into that realm is the Country Music Hall of Fame at 4 Music Square East. The tour is a self-guided one that can take as little or as much time as you like, but give yourself at least an hour.

Among the most interesting of the galleries is the "Styles of Country Music" exhibit. Here, the visitor begins to understand how bluegrass, Cajun, cowboy, honky-tonk, western swing, rockabilly and contemporary all go together to make up country. And one begins to see why "country music" is so hard to pin down and define.

Another display proves that you just never can predict when inspiration will hit you. Throughout the gallery are the words and sometimes the music to hit songs—all scribbled on napkins, hotel stationery, even real estate forms.

Of course, the actual Country Music Hall of Fame is in the

145

building as well. It is here that the greats of country music are honored on brass plaques that line the walls of the rooms.

The Hall of Fame is open daily from 9 a.m. to 5 p.m. September through May and from 8 a.m. to 7 p.m. June through August. It is closed on Thanksgiving, Christmas and New Year's Day.

Admission is $7.50 for adults and $2 for children.

For a taste of the other side of Nashville, visit one of the city's many art galleries or museums.

One you'll want to include is the Carol Van Vechten Gallery at Fisk University, which houses the Stieglitz Collection, donated by Georgia O'Keeffe. There are more than 100 works—by the likes of Picasso, Cezanne and Renoir—in the collection. The gallery is open from 10 a.m. to 5 p.m. Tuesday through Friday and from 1 to 5 p.m. Saturday and Sunday.

Admission is free, but donations of $4 for adults and $2 for children are suggested.

The Cumberland Science Museum, with its planetarium and live science demonstrations and animal shows daily, is an excellent stop for the grown-ups and the children.

The museum is open Monday through Saturday from 9:30 a.m. to 5 p.m. and from 12:30 to 5:30 p.m. Sunday, June through August. From September through May, the hours are the same, but the museum is closed on Monday.

Admission is $5 for adults and $4 for children.

More to See and Do

Nashville Zoo. More than 800 animals are housed on 50 acres where the exhibits are designed to duplicate the animals' natural environments. Open Memorial Day to Labor Day 9 a.m. to 6 p.m. The rest of the year, hours are 10 a.m. to 5 p.m. Admission is $5 for adults and $3 for senior citizens and children.

Hatch Show Print. One of the oldest poster-print shops in America. Hatch has been in business since 1879. The company still uses the same technique for its present-day posters that it did at the start. Open Monday through Friday from 10 a.m. to 5 p.m. Visitors are welcome.

How to Get There
Nashville is in north central Tennessee on I-65.

Where to Stay
Courtyard by Marriott. Non-smoking rooms available.

The Hermitage. Set in an historic hotel. Non-smoking rooms available.

Union Station. Set in renovated 1897 train station. Non-smoking rooms available.

Camping is available at Nashville KOA, Two Rivers Campground, Holiday Nashville Travel Park and Fiddlers Inn Campground.

Where to Eat
Elliston Place Soda Shop. Part of Nashville since 1939. Serves breakfast, lunch and dinner.

The Merchants. Downtown restaurant in an historic building. Specializes in fresh grilled meat and seafood. Serves lunch during the week and dinner daily.

For More Information
For more information about Nashville, call 1-615-259-4755.

ABOUT THE AUTHOR

Lynn Edge started her writing career as a general assignment reporter for The Birmingham News. For the last two decades she has been a free-lance writer, contributing to newspapers and magazines thbroughout the United States.

She is author of four other books, *And To Y'all A Good Night*, a bed and breakfast guide to Alabama, *Shoals to Sand Dunes*, an exhaustive travel guide to Alabama, *Chilton County Peaches*, a specialty cookbook targeting Alabama's most famous fruit crop, and *Planting & Growing in Alabama*, a guide to regional gardening. She also is co-author of a travel guide on the Mississippi coast, entitled *Ramblin' and Gamblin' on the Mississippi Coast*.

Ms. Edge is married and has two children. She and her family live in Birmingham.